Steven Truscott

Decades of Injustice

by Nate Hendley

D1065597

FIVE RIVERS PUBLISHING
WWW.5RIVERS.ORG

Published by Five Rivers Publishing, 704 Queen Street, P.O. Box 293, Neustadt, ON N0G 2M0, Canada www.5rivers.org

Steven Truscott: Decades of Injustice, Copyright © 2012 by Nate Hendley.

Edited by Lorina Stephens.

Cover by Lorina Stephens, Copyright © 2012 by Five Rivers Publishing.

Interior design and layout by Lorina Stephens

Text set in Arno Pro

Title set in Brittannic Bold

Headers and sub-titles set in

Published in Canada

Library and Archives Canada Cataloguing in Publication

Hendley, Nate

Steven Truscott : decades of injustice / Nate Hendley.

Includes bibliographical references.

Issued also in electronic format.

ISBN 978-1-927400-21-0

1. Truscott, Steven, 1945-. 2. Murder--Ontario--Clinton. 3. Trials (Murder)--Ontario--Goderich. 4. Judicial error--Ontario. I. Title.

HV6535.C33C55 2012a 364.152'30971322 C2012-905895-5

This book is dedicated to the Truscott family, for enduring and believing.

Contents

Chapter One: Getting to Know Steven Truscott

June 9/1959

6:30 pm

Steven Truscott leisurely biked around the grounds of Air Vice Marshal Hugh Campbell School—the main academic institute for young children whose parents worked at the Clinton Royal Canadian Air Force base. It was a humid night—Clinton was in the midst of a heat-wave and it hadn't rained in a month. Truscott wiped his brow and vaguely thought about going swimming or fishing. A good-looking 14 year-old boy, Truscott had brown hair slicked down in the style of the day. He wore red pants and had a green bike. Tall for his age, Steven exuded the confident air of an adventurous teenager who loved sports and being outdoors. The previous

November, he led his school football team to victory in a competition called the Little Grey Cup.

There were no planes at this RCAF installation; it served as a teaching center, where air force men and women studied radar, radio, meteorology and telegraphy, among other disciplines. The base was located a few kilometres from Clinton, a small, conservative community in southwestern Ontario. Three hours west of Toronto and minutes away from Lake Huron, Clinton was a dry town, with no beer or liquor stores.

At its peak, the RCAF base accommodated 3,000 personnel. Among their ranks was Truscott's father, Daniel, an RCAF warrant officer. His mother Doris largely devoted herself to looking after her boisterous family, which included first-born son Ken (who was 16) and two siblings, Bill and Barbara who were younger than Steven. The family lived at 2 Quebec Road in the Permanent Married Quarters (PMQs) on the base. The PMQs was a community within a community for RCAF members with families. Single enlisted RCAF personnel had to make do with barracks.

While Steven Truscott was popular with his peers, he was wary about getting too attached to any one particular set of friends. As an army brat, he had moved with his family from base to base across the country, at the direction of army prerogatives. The Truscott family had been living at RCAF base Clinton since the summer of 1956.

Truscott was due back home at 8:30 pm, to babysit his little brother and sister. In the meantime, he took advantage of the unseasonal warmth by roaming. Most of the other kids in the base PMQs had the same idea, and the evening air was filled with the sounds of children at play. Adults also enjoyed the fine weather, firing up barbeques or just sitting outside, cold drinks in hand.

Truscott, seen in this early and undated photo, was sentence to hang in 1959 for the murder of 12-year-old Lynne Harper.
(Canadian Press)

Truscott continued his somewhat aimless rambling. He biked away from A.V.M. Hugh Campbell School, towards the county road, the main thoroughfare in the community. The paved, two-lane county road led north from the RCAF base. The road bordered the property of Bob Lawson, a local farmer. He owned 150 acres of farm and brush directly east of the county road. Bob was a genial man and local children liked to hang out at his property, to play and watch the farm animals. Kids also frequented a wooded patch called Lawson's Bush set on the northern end of his property. Lawson's Bush could be directly accessed from the county road by a rough lane known colloquially as the tractor trail.

"The Lawson's were really nice to us ..." Joan Tyre recalled, decades later, in a police interview. "We were like their kids. We could go and look at the cows. They had a big barn and they had a radio up there so we'd go and listen to all the latest dance tunes. It was just fun."

Like Truscott, Tyre grew up on the RCAF Clinton base in the late 1950s.

Several hundred feet past Lawson's Bush, the Canadian National Railway tracks crossed the county road. And just a short distance from the tracks was the Bayfield River, which was a popular spot to swim and fish on hot days. The county road followed a bridge over this river and led to King's Highway 8, a major roadway. To the west, King's Highway 8 led to Clinton. To the east, it led to the town of Seaforth.

Truscott was seen biking around the bridge over the Bayfield River by a handful of people, including Beatrice Geiger, an air force base mom out for a bike ride of her own. At some point, Truscott bicycled back to the school grounds, where a pack of Brownies were having a scavenger hunt. Truscott causally watched the Brownies, in no great hurry to get home. A young girl named Lynne Harper, who had been chatting with one of the adults supervising the Brownies, noticed Truscott and sauntered over. At 12 years-old, Harper was a petite (five foot three, 100 pound) schoolgirl in the same mixed grade seven and eight class at A.V. M. Hugh Campbell to which Truscott belonged. Her family also lived in the PMQs section of the RCAF base. She wore turquoise shorts and a white blouse.

Harper walked up to Truscott, who stood by his bike, and began bantering with him. She sat on his front bike tire as they causally made small talk. At some point, the girl made a request.

"I was going towards [the Bayfield River] to see some of the boys who were going fishing," Truscott recounted later in a statement to police. "She asked if she could have a ride down to the highway."

Truscott said sure, and the pair strolled away from the

playground. Truscott, who was walking his bike, looked inside a kindergarten classroom and spotted a clock, which read 7:25 pm. Once the pair reached the county road, Harper seated herself on the crossbars of Truscott's bike and he gave her a ride to the highway.

Truscott said Harper asked him about a little white house outside of town where a local recluse lived. The recluse raised ponies and local children liked to go out to his house to look at them. Harper seemed in a buoyant mood, even if she admitted to quarrelling with her parents, recalled Truscott.

"She said she was mad at her mother 'cause she didn't let her go swimming. That is all she said on the way down. She wasn't mad. She was care-free. It took about three or four minutes. She just asked if she could get off and she got off and I went back to the bridge," Truscott told police.

He estimated he dropped her off around 7:30 pm.

Truscott said he stopped on the bridge to look back at his passenger. He noticed that Harper was hitchhiking by the side of the highway.

"I just turned around to see if she had a ride yet and a grey Chev picked her up. She had her thumb out. A car swerved in off (the) edge of the road and pulled out," stated Truscott.

The vehicle stopped on the side of the highway, giving Truscott a good opportunity to examine it. He noticed "an odd licence plate" on the vehicle, which he further identified as a 1959 model. The plate in question had a yellow background. Like many teenage boys, Truscott was a car buff. He cited several pertinent details about the Chevrolet in his police statement.

The car had "quite a bit of chrome, white wall tires … it was something like a Bel Air," read his statement to police.

According to Truscott, Harper "got in the front seat and the car pulled away, going towards Seaforth … I just stayed down at the bridge and watched boys swimming then went back to the school. Boys were (Arnold) George, (Doug) Oates, (Jerry) Durnin, (Garry) Gilks (sic). On the way down I waved to (the) boys. On way back I waved at Arnold George, a school chum. I stopped for about five minutes. The boys were about 150 feet away … I stayed at the bridge about five minutes. I didn't see the car again. I looked at (the) highway once and didn't see anything."

Truscott proceeded to bike home, past the school grounds where some kids were still playing. Truscott got off his bicycle and mingled with the boys, whose ranks included Ken, his older brother.

Eleven-year-old Stewart Westie, a grade seven student at the school, was one of several children who saw Truscott upon his return. Westie was playing baseball that night and importantly, was wearing a watch.

"I saw Steve and Lynn (sic) about 7:30 pm but I would allow 20 minutes either way," read Westie's statement to police. "The first I saw them they were walking between the white fence and the school, Steve pushing the bike and Lynn (sic) walking beside him. They walked up past the school and right up the county road just above the bend, and then Lynn (sic) got on the bike and Steven got on and they rode in the direction of the river. I didn't see them talking. I just turned and saw them going up. We were playing baseball. About half an hour later Steven came down the road on his bicycle alone

... one of the boys called to him, 'What did you do with Lynn (sic), feed her to the fishes?' and Steve said, 'No. I just let her off at the highway.'"

A few other teasing remarks were made then Ken reminded his sibling that it was his turn to babysit. Ken, who was riding Billy's bicycle, suggested that he and Steve change bikes. This was done, and Truscott rode home, on his younger brother's bike. He got in around 8:25 pm, according to his mother who was chatting with a neighbour. It was still remarkably warm and light out. The sun would not set until 9:08 that evening.

Truscott's parents left the house shortly after their second-born son arrived. Steven checked the refrigerator to see if there was anything good to eat. He selected some food then prepared for an uneventful evening of babysitting.

Chapter Two: Getting to Know Lynne Harper

Flying Officer Leslie Harper, his wife, Shirley, and their three children, lived on 15 Victoria Boulevard in the Permanent Married Quarters (PMQs) of RCAF Station Clinton. Their 12 year-old daughter, Lynne, was the middle child in the family. Born in 1946, her full name was Cheryl Lynne Harper. In June 1959, she had a 16-year-old brother named Barry and a five year-old brother named Jeffrey.

The Harper home had a large lawn and was shaded by trees in both front and back. The lawn was kept orderly and trim (army regulations demanded frequent mowing and maintenance). Clean-cut Lynne was active in Girl Guides and enjoyed helping around her home. Her mother had rheumatism in her hands, so Harper frequently assisted with household chores. By all accounts, Harper was eager to be liked and accepted.

Until You Are Dead—author Julian Sher's brilliant account of the Truscott story— quotes one Maynard Cory on this aspect of Harper's personality. Cory was the proprietor of a convenience store on the RCAF base that was patronized by kids in the area.

Cory described Harper as a "tiny little thing ... I guess you notice people who wanted to be noticed, and she wanted to be noticed. She was pretty in a plain way. Kind of coquettish. You couldn't help but like her."

Joan Tyre went to the same school as Harper, but was two years older than the girl. In a 2005 police interview, Tyre recalled what Harper was like.

"Lynne used to come over to our house even though she was younger. We'd have parties in our basement and she'd want to come so sometime I'd invite her ... but you know when you're 14 and she's 12—it's kind of a big age difference ... we were friends, but we didn't hang out a lot together," Tyre told police.

"She just wanted to belong. She wanted to do what the other kids did and not so much the little kids but more the older kids. She just wanted to have a friend ... I don't know if she got a lot of attention at home ... I don't think she got a lot of attention because she was very, I don't know, clingy. She wanted to be with the bigger kids," continued Tyre.

On June 9, 1959, Lynne Harper left the RCAF base with some other girls to play baseball.

"Lynne was on my team," said Tyre. "She hit the ball and she didn't run fast enough so she didn't make it to first base. So I gave her heck. I said Lynne, you run like an old lady and she goes well, I'm going home. She started to cry and she left and I thought, oh great, you know, here we are off base. I'm going to get in trouble for this."

Harper apparently recovered her composure. She left the ball game and returned home. At 5:30 pm, she ate a turkey dinner. Once dinner was done, Harper got into an argument with her parents. She wanted to go swimming at the pool on the RCAF base. Problem was, as a minor, she required adult supervision or a military pass to swim there. Harper went off to see if she could secure a pass from a base official but failed. She returned home in a huff, did the dishes then left the house again around 6:15 pm. She did not tell her parents where she was headed.

In addition to her turquoise shorts, white blouse and brown shoes, Harper wore a locket around her neck with an RCAF crest on it. The locket had been a recent present from an aunt.

Harper walked up Victoria Boulevard and Winnipeg Road in the PMQs. Then she went north to a park area by A.V.M. Hugh Campbell School. She arrived at the school grounds at 6:30 pm. A Brownie meeting was going on, and Harper eagerly joined in a scavenger hunt. Harper helped organize the little girls and chatted with an adult Brownie leader named Anne Nickerson.

"Lynn (sic) asked if she could stay, and about 6:40 pm, I sat down under a tree and talked with Lynn (sic)," said Anne Nickerson in her police statement. "She said she didn't want to go home, her mother was cross with her ... I must have talked with her about 20 minutes. At about five after seven Lynn (sic) walked away and then a boy came along with red trousers and red shirt on. He had a bike and parked it and Lynne sat on the side. I didn't know the boy, not by name, but by sight, and now believe it to have been Stephen Truscott (sic). They walked away together ... him pushing the bike."

This was not the first time Harper had approached Truscott. A few days earlier at a house party for local teens, the grade seven student had walked up to Truscott and asked him to dance. Truscott accepted and the two cut a few steps. All witnesses to the event stated that this was the full extent of their intimacy.

Now, at the school grounds, Harper had another request. According to Truscott, she wanted a ride down to Highway 8. She idly mentioned something about maybe seeing some ponies owned by a recluse who lived in a white house outside town. Several witnesses, including Nickerson, saw Harper and Truscott walk off together. When they reached the county road, Harper seated herself on Truscott's handle bars and the two descended toward the highway.

Several children would tell police that the pair passed them on the county road, heading to the highway. These children included Richard Gellatly and Truscott's close friend, Arnold "Butch" George. A boy named Dougie Oates, busy digging for turtles by the Bayfield River, said he saw the two as they cleared the bridge over the lazy waterway. Another boy, named Gordon Logan, was swimming a few hundred feet from the bridge. According to his account, he was standing on a rock when he observed Harper and Truscott bicycle by on the bridge. A few minutes later, he saw Truscott bike back alone. Logan thought nothing more about this and continued to swim.

Truscott would tell police he dropped Harper off at Highway 8 and saw her get into a car. He gave police the brand and colour of the vehicle. The assumption was she was hitchhiking.

That evening, Leslie and Barry Harper searched fruitlessly around the PMQs for Lynne. At 11:15 pm, Harper contacted his neighbour, Flight Sergeant Frank Johnson, who belonged to the base police. Ten minutes later, Flying Officer Harper called the RCAF guardhouse. Corporal William Webb was on duty. Harper explained to Webb that his daughter was missing. Harper suggested his daughter might have hitchhiked to see her grandmother in Port Stanley (about 80 miles away) after having a family quarrel. A few minutes after the call, Corporal Webb contacted the Ontario Provincial Police in Exeter, ON. The OPP issued a report stating that 12 year-old Lynne Harper was a runaway who was most likely hitch-hiking.

Back at 15 Victoria Boulevard, the worried Harper parents left the house lights on and door unlocked, for their tardy daughter.

Leslie and Shirley Harper weren't the only people in the area having a disquieting evening. After sundown, farmer Bob Lawson had a surprise visitor at his farmhouse. His neighbour Ross Kreitch showed up at his house and suggested the pair go swimming in the Bayfield River. It was still humid out and Lawson was game. The two climbed into Lawson's car and traveled down the county road towards the Bayfield River. As they drove, they spotted something unusual.

"There was a car that was parked next to the bush, on the east side of the road, probably about 75 feet south of the tractor trail," Lawson would later testify before the Ontario Court of Appeal. "It was a convertible, maroon or red Ford convertible, and there was one person in it for sure and probably two."

Lawson had never seen a car parked in this locale so late at night. The convertible was such an unusual sight, Lawson decided to investigate—or rather, to cause mischief.

"We pulled up behind them and shone the lights on them … just to irritate them, I guess," he told the Court of Appeal.

The driver in the convertible didn't react in any way, so Lawson backed up and drove off. He parked his own vehicle by the north end of the bridge. The hard-working farmer and his friend, Krietch, went for a night-time swim. At some point, the mystery car made another appearance, this time in motion, tearing up the county road.

"It sped past us at one point and the person in it yelled some obscenities at us, I think, but I don't recall what he said … he was headed north. Come across the bridge. He was headed north," Lawson recalled.

Lawson would report his odd experience at the guardhouse on the RCAF base. But by then, authorities were concerned with other matters that seemed more urgent than a farmer's late night encounter with a strange car.

Chapter Three: The Rape and Murder of Lynne Harper

Leslie Harper was worried. It was the morning of June 10 and Lynne still hadn't returned home. Around 7:30 am, Flying Officer Harper drove to the RCAF base and started asking around about his daughter. One of the people he approached was Daniel Truscott. Harper wanted to know if any of Truscott's kids had seen Lynne. Truscott wasn't sure, so he suggested Harper stop by his house and check for himself. It was 7:45 am and Dan Truscott didn't think his children had left for school yet.

Doris Truscott was home when Leslie Harper knocked on the side door of her house. Harper explained his mission and asked if any of the Truscott kids had seen Lynne. Ken Truscott, who was shining his shoes, said no. Steven, who was finishing breakfast, said yes, he had seen her. In fact, he had given her a ride on his bike to Highway 8 the night before. The last time he saw Lynne, she was getting into a grey Chevrolet by the side of the road.

Harper blanched when he heard this and left. Flying Officer Harper and his wife, Shirley, began calling Lynne's friends to see if she had spent the night with them. The answer in each case was "no".

At the Ontario Provincial Police (OPP) station in Goderich, ON, Constable Donald Hobbs was going on duty when he read a notice about Lynne Harper being missing. Constable Hobbs drove to RCAF Station Clinton to see if he could help in any way. The policeman met with Flying Officer Harper at the RCAF guardhouse. Harper gave the constable a description of his daughter and told him what Steven Truscott had said about dropping her by the highway.

Around 9:15 am, Constable Hobbs and Sergeant Frank Johnson, of the RCAF police, arrived at Daniel Truscott's workplace. They asked Warrant Officer Truscott to come with them as they drove to A.V.M. Hugh Campbell School. Dan Truscott was asked to fetch his son from class. This was done, and soon Steven Truscott was in the front passenger seat of the police cruiser, talking with Constable Hobbs. Steven's father sat in the back with Sergeant Johnson. Truscott began what would be the first of countless recitations of his activities from the previous evening. Truscott was under no legal obligation to provide any information. He hadn't been placed under arrest, which meant his presence in the police car was entirely voluntary. It's not clear if Steven and his father were aware of this, however. The notion of civil rights was hazy at the time and people in general—particularly in the military—were very respectful of authority. Police were also under much less scrutiny then they are today. In the late 1950s, Canadian police weren't required to tell a suspect what their rights were during questioning or even during an arrest.

The end-result was that unless police told them otherwise, it's likely neither Steven nor his father realized they could have ended the interview at any time and exited the car.

The police spoke to Truscott for a few minutes then the boy returned to class. Naturally, all the kids at the school were talking about Harper's disappearance. It was assumed she had hitch-hiked somewhere and would be in big trouble when she was found. Some of the children remembered that Truscott was the last person to see the girl. The kids teased Truscott, asking if he and Harper were an item.

The day the police arrived, the A.V.M. Hugh Campbell School was having a half-holiday, to mark the Clinton Fair. Ken and Steven were among a dozen or so boys who spent the afternoon swimming at a quarry west of Clinton. When police arrived at the Truscott home after lunch, Steven wasn't there. OPP Constable Donald Trumbley and RCAF Corporal Keith Lipscombe came back at 5 pm, by which time Steven had returned. They drove Steven and Doris out to the bridge over the Bayfield River.

Constable Trumbley asked Steven to show him where he had been standing when he looked back and saw Harper at the highway. Doris remained in the car. The policeman and Corporal Lipscombe stood next to Steven and watched cars go by on Highway 8.

Truscott and Doris were brought back home, but the police

weren't done with them yet. At 8:00 pm, Ontario Provincial Police Sergeant Charles Anderson from Goderich showed up at the Truscott household. Police were intensely curious about Steven's actions on the night of June 9. He was, after all, the last person seen with a now missing girl. Whether he knew it or not, Steven had become a prime suspect in Lynne Harper's disappearance. The sergeant wanted Steven to show him the route he took to Highway 8 with Lynne. Once again, Steven and his mother obliged. The boy retraced his steps for the sergeant, from the school and down the county road. When asked, Steven denied he'd ever dated Harper or given her a bike ride before the fateful evening in question. Once the police were finally done with their questions, Truscott and his friend Arnold "Butch" George and some other boys walked to the bridge over the Bayfield River. There, they hung out. There was much talk of Harper's disappearance and some ribbing of Steven. He was teased about being seen with a girl. His friends wanted to know if he had taken Harper into the bush.

That evening, police began pulling over cars with yellow or orange licence plates. There was no sense of panic yet in the community, however. The weather was still very warm and the Clinton Fair was in full swing.

On June 11, Truscott was taken out of class around noon for yet more questioning by police, without his mother or father present. This was all perfectly legal. At the time, Canadian law did not stipulate that juveniles had to have a parent present when interviewed by police. Policemen began interviewing other children from the school in an empty room. During his interrogation, Constable Hobbs asked Truscott if he had left anything out of his story. It turned out, he had. Truscott remembered seeing a gold chain locket with an RCAF crest on it, around Harper's neck. Truscott was asked to list anyone who might have seen him with Harper. Truscott offered up several names: his friend Arnold George, Dougie Oates and Richard Gellatly.

Truscott seemed unruffled by all the attention from police. Stoicism was the Truscott's preferred mode of expression, as befitting a military family.

Later that morning, a search party of 250 RCAF men organized at the request of police, came together at the base. The group was tasked with searching for a body—a concession that Harper might already be dead. The team was divided up into three. One search party combed the banks of the Bayfield River, another examined the area near Highway 8 while a third investigated farmer Bob Lawson's property. The searchers started their mission around 1:00 pm.

Corporal George Edens and another man were working Lawson's Bush under the command of Flying Officer Glen Sage. Thirty minutes into the search, Corporal Edens and his partner made a discovery—Harper's body. According to Sage's later statement to police, one of the men shouted "Here she is!" and a call went down the line of searchers that Harper had been found. Flying Officer Sage rushed forward and took charge of the situation. He ordered the other searchers to stay back from the site, to preserve the crime scene.

Harper's corpse was found lying in a hollow, set in a woodlot containing maple and ash trees, a little over 80 feet from the tractor trail. She was on her back and even a cursory inspection would indicate she had been sexually assaulted. Sweltering under the heat of another hot day, Harper's remains teemed with maggots. Her right arm was still in her blouse, which was otherwise knotted around her neck. She was naked from the waist down.

In his official police report, OPP officer Hank Sayeau wrote: "The body, partly concealed by tree branches, was lying face up in a east-westerly direction, with the head being to the east at a point 82 feet south of the fence bounding the woods on the north and 351 feet, two inches, east of the fence bounding the woods on the west. It was clad only in an undershirt while an instrument, later found to be a blouse, was knotted around the neck. A pair of blue shorts, a pair of white socks and a pair of brown loafer shoes were lying at the extended right elbow, a pair of underpanties were 33 feet, eight inches north easterly from the body. The scene gave every indication of murder and rape."

In an odd touch, three branches from ash saplings had been broken off about two meters from the ground, and laid diagonally across Harper's body. Equally perplexing was the fact her clothing—as noted by Officer Sayeau—had been neatly folded next to her body. Her socks were rolled up and her shorts zippered and placed carefully on the ground, as if the killer were concerned with appearances. Her panties had no rips or tears in them. Given that they were found ten meters from Harper's body, it appeared her killer had dropped them by accident while moving her body.

The presence of neatly folded clothes indicated the killer took their time in the woods. This suggested a psychopath, someone who was cool enough to tidy up a murder scene before departing. A rapist-killer more bothered by unravelled socks than the presence of a corpse.

There was no indication of a struggle at the death scene and no evidence of footprints either. The lack of prints indicated the killer was either very cautious or simply that the ground was too dry to record the imprint of a shoe. There was very little blood on or near the girl's body. Even the turf around Harper was largely undisturbed. Some of the stunned searchers removed their jackets and chivalrously placed them over the dead girl's body, to preserve modesty after death.

The first policeman on the scene was Corporal Sayeau, who arrived at 2:08 pm. He was joined a few minutes later by Constable Donald Trumbley. Police removed the jackets that had been placed over Harper and handed them back to their owners. In doing so, police committed the first of several procedural errors. The jackets were not checked to see if they had picked up blood, hair or fingerprints from the body.

Police searched in vain for clues. They could find no fingerprints on Harper's clothes and body, or on the tree branches placed over her corpse. Some marks beneath Harper's feet were noted, but no one was sure if they were footprints or not. In any case, no cast was made of these marks. More visible were marks on Harper herself, including a scratch on the front of her left leg that went from above her knee to nearly her toes.

Dr. David Hall Brooks, a medical officer at the RCAF base, arrived the crime scene and confirmed that the victim was Lynne Harper. Dr. Brooks lived across the street from the girl's family, and knew Lynne by sight. This was a small mercy for the girl's parents, for it meant they would not be required to view the corpse in the woods to confirm it was their daughter.

Police and RCAF personnel alike were shocked. Huron

County was a low-crime area. Violent murders, let alone sex murders, just simply didn't happen in the community.

Corporal John Erskine, district identification officer with the OPP, took photographs of the death scene and made various measurements.

Around 2:35 pm, a coroner from Clinton arrived at the scene. He did nothing, however, because Dr. Brooks was already present. Soon, the physicians were joined by a third medical man: Dr. John Penistan, the Stratford, ON-based pathologist for the area. After arriving on site, Dr. Penistan was briefed on the situation by Dr. Brooks.

Dr. Penistan carefully examined Harper's corpse. The doctor took samples from the small amount of blood that could be found on the remains and made note of the maggots festering on the girl. The pathologist spent about one hour inspecting the death scene. When the doctor was through, Harper's body was carried out of the woods on a stretcher and taken to the Ball and Hutch Funeral Home in Clinton.

Back at Lawson's Bush, Edens—the same man who discovered Harper's body—came across a fresh set of car tire tracks near the tractor trail that led into Lawson's Bush. The skid marks were in roughly the same area where the mystery car seen by farmer Lawson had been. There were some old bicycle track marks in the same spot. The RCAF men reported their finding to police, who duly noted the suspicious marks.

At 7:15 pm, in a room at the Ball and Hutch Funeral Home, Dr. Penistan and Dr. Brooks (who took notes) began the most important autopsy of their careers. Three police officers stood in the tiny room, watching. Dr. Penistan would have preferred to have done the autopsy in Stratford, where he had proper equipment and space. But no matter; police wanted the autopsy done as quickly as possible.

The less than ideal conditions were noted by Dr. Penistan himself in a May 19, 1966 memo he wrote to OPP officials: "The autopsy was carried out in the preparation room of the Ball and Hutch Funeral Home in Clinton. This measured about 13 feet x 8 feet and was equipped with a white enamelled table measuring 6 feet six inches and having a three foot high rim ... light from an overhead bulb was inadequate and was supplemented by a standard lamp which was brought in on request. Floor space was limited, impeding freedom of movement for laying out instruments and equipment for collecting specimens was inadequate."

At one point, the two doctors opened up Harper's stomach and removed samples of its contents, which they placed in a glass jar. Dr. Penistan held the jar up to the light to take a closer look. Working on the assumption that a normal stomach took two hours to digest a meal, Dr. Penistan gauged the amount of food in the girl's body with the degree of putrefaction in the corpse, and decided she died two hours after eating her last meal. If Harper ate supper at 5:30 pm on June 9, then she most likely died sometime between 7:15 and 7:45 pm that same night, said the doctor. The cause of death was strangulation.

What Dr. Penistan didn't find during the autopsy was equally revealing. While it was obvious Harper had been sexually assaulted in some way, it wasn't clear if she had actually been raped. Dr. Penistan couldn't find any traces of semen on her (or at the crime scene either). He did discover lots of acid phosphatase, an enzyme found in male semen, but not an enzyme manufactured by women. Or so the doctor believed. Dr. Penistan's assumptions about acid phosphatase would be critically challenged by future medical experts when Truscott's case came up for review.

At the same time the makeshift autopsy was being held, Inspector Harold Graham of the Criminal Investigative Branch of the OPP arrived from police headquarters in Toronto. A storied officer with a solid reputation as a no-nonsense cop, Graham would be involved in dozens of murder cases during his career. He showed up in Clinton at 7:45 pm charged with a single mission: solve the Harper case, fast. It was not just that the crime was awful and that a vicious sex criminal remained at large. The case strained the always touchy relationship between Clinton and the military base. People in base and town alike hoped the killer didn't come from their ranks.

Chapter Four: The Investigation and Arrest of Steven Truscott

The day Lynne Harper was found in Lawson's Bush, the Ontario Provincial Police (OPP) issued a General Information Broadcast to update their colleagues about the case. The alert said Harper had been "raped and strangled" and urged police to be on the lookout for suspects with "scratches on face, neck, hands and arms". The assumption was that Harper had struggled with her killer.

No original copies of this alert can be found in police files, only a hand-written copy penned by Inspector Harold Graham. Interestingly, Graham got his dates mixed up, stating that Harper had likely been murdered Tuesday, June 10 "around 9 pm."

While getting the days of the week confused might have been an honest mistake, Inspector Graham's estimated time of death was more problematic for investigators. At 9 pm on the night Harper was murdered, Steven Truscott was at home watching television. Nor did police notice any visible scratches on Truscott's face or hands. It is likely for these reasons that Inspector Graham's hand-written copy of the alert disappeared into police files, not to emerge until decades later.

Provincial alerts aside, the police focused most of their attention on a single suspect, Steven Truscott. There was virtually no physical evidence that tied Truscott to the case. His fingerprints weren't found at the crime scene, or shoe prints, or bits of his clothes, hair or blood. Evidence of any of the latter would be conclusive proof that Truscott took the girl into the woods. While all the evidence against Truscott was circumstantial, police seemed convinced they'd found their suspect.

While focused, repetitive questioning of suspects is standard police procedure, law officials displayed intense myopia in their treatment of Truscott. Future investigations would reveal other suspects with far shadier pasts than 14 year-old Steven, but these leads were dropped after police decided they had their killer.

At 10:45 am on June 12, Steven Truscott was called out of class once again by police. Inspector Graham himself wanted to meet the boy. Daniel Truscott accompanied his son as Steven spoke to police. Inspector Graham wanted a detailed recounting of Truscott's encounter with Harper. Truscott's comments (but very few of the questions put to him by police) were recorded by RCAF base stenographer Dorene Jervis. When asked about this later at trial, Inspector

Graham offered two reasons why he didn't instruct Jervis to take down most of his questions. Graham said he didn't know how proficient Jervis was at shorthand and feared she might not be fast enough to accurately record both questions and answers. Besides, Truscott wasn't actually a suspect at the time—merely a witness, the inspector told the court. Both statements seem flippant at best. Steven Truscott was weary of the repeated police inquiries, but remained polite and focused. Truscott repeated his story of taking Harper to the highway on his bike. He denied having any romantic interest in the girl. Inspector Graham asked a few more questions then let the boy go. Truscott's initial encounter with the high-ranking Toronto officer had lasted 20 minutes.

Inspector Graham interviewed other children at the school: Dougie Oates, Arnold "Butch" George and a young girl named Jocelyne Gaudet. George and Oates both said they saw Harper and Truscott together on the bridge over the Bayfield River. Gaudet spoke of wandering around the tractor trail on the evening of June 9 in an unsuccessful search for Harper. Her story would evolve over the next 24 hours into a much more convoluted tale. Her confused memories would have a devastating impact on Steven Truscott.

While Graham interviewed children, Corporal Hank Sayeau transported the sealed jar containing Harper's stomach contents to the Ontario attorney-general's laboratory in Toronto. At the lab, the contents of the jar were examined first by biologist John Funk then by Dr. Noble Sharpe, who was the latter's medical director. Later that afternoon, Corporal Sayeau checked in with the crime lab.

Funk spoke with the constable, relaying Dr. Sharpe's

observations. Whatever Funk said, he didn't include a precise time of death. It is likely Funk offered a very preliminary prognosis that Harper might have died shortly after eating. Corporal Sayeau proceeded to call Inspector Graham in Goderich to report the lab's findings. Somehow in the course of these communications, police decided the laboratory had confirmed Dr. John Penistan's estimated time of death. Inspector Graham now believed he had medical proof Harper died within two hours of eating, between 7:15 and 7:45 pm. The only person known to be with Harper during this time was Steven Truscott. The inspector thought he had his man or boy as the case may be.

"I instructed Constable (Donald) Trumbley to locate Steven Truscott and to ask him to accompany him to the Provincial Police office at Goderich (preferably alone)," Inspector Graham would later explain in a police statement.

The Constable found Truscott shortly before 7:00 pm on Bob Lawson's farm. When Trumbley pulled up at the gate to the farm, Truscott was ambling home. Trumbley asked Truscott to accompany him to the OPP station in Goderich, ON, to go over his statement. Truscott was agreeable and got into the cruiser. The pair arrived at the Goderich detachment at 7:40 pm. Shortly after, Inspector Graham arrived. Doris and Daniel Truscott had not been invited to join in. Police were again taking advantage of the fact they weren't required to have a parent present when questioning a juvenile.

Inspector Graham outlined what happened next in his police statement: "At 7:50 pm in the presence of Constable Trumbley, I told Steven Truscott that Mrs. Jervis had typed out the conversation he had with me in the office earlier that day, and I asked him to read it aloud and very carefully, to be sure that it was as he had spoken and to make any changes or corrections he wished. He did read the statement aloud and said it was correct with the exception of one time which he said should be 7:50 or 7:55 pm rather than 8 pm. This was changed. He said it was correct and he signed the statement."

Truscott might have thought that was all the police wanted. In fact, they had some new questions. Inspector Graham had spoken at length with Jocelyne Gaudet throughout the day. Gaudet was now saying Truscott tried to make a date with her to go into Lawson's Bush to see some calves. Gaudet said Truscott had come around to her house at 5:50 pm on June 9 to remind her of their date in the bush. Gaudet apparently couldn't make it, so Truscott left without her..

When Inspector Graham related this to his prime suspect, Truscott denied it. The Toronto OPP officer made it clear he didn't believe Truscott. Police believed Truscott had taken Harper into Lawson's Bush then assaulted and killed her, leaving her body behind. Inspector Graham would later say that two pieces of evidence convinced him of Truscott's guilt: the medical examination of Harper's stomach contents and Gaudet's statements. In the inspector's mind, the stomach content analysis proved that Harper died shortly after encountering Truscott. Gaudet's testimony, meanwhile, revealed that Truscott was a budding pervert, eager to lure young girls into the woods. If he couldn't be with Gaudet in Lawson's Bush, then he'd settle for Harper. Or so, Inspector Graham believed.

Inspector Graham questioned Truscott for nearly 90 minutes with the assistance of Constable Trumbley. They did not make an official record of the interrogation. Graham took a single page of notes during the hour-and-a-half session. There was no stenographer present, or a tape recorder, much less a lawyer or Truscott's parents. In fact, police didn't even inform Truscott's mother or father than their son had been taken in for questioning.

The policemen worked Truscott over in turns. One man would question the boy while the other left the room. Then the second man would come in and take over the interrogation. Police wanted Truscott to admit to raping and murdering Harper. The boy refused to oblige and stuck to his story about biking Harper to the highway. Throughout the ordeal, Truscott didn't cry or break down, remaining true to his family's stoic code.

After unsuccessfully attempting to get the boy to confess, Inspector Graham and Constable Trumbley drove Truscott back to the guardhouse at the RCAF base. It was around 9:30 pm at night.

In Clinton, Daniel and Doris Truscott were extremely worried. Steven hadn't come home for dinner and now he was missing. Did the same killer who abducted and murdered Lynne Harper strike again?

Inspector Graham related what happened next in his official report: "We took Steven back to the guardhouse on the RCAF base and at 9:30, Sgt. (Charles) Anderson left the guardhouse to make arrangements for the boy's father to come to the guardhouse."

Truscott would later deny this was the case, and said his father had to find out on his own where his son was being held. Regardless, once Daniel Truscott got word his son was at the RCAF guardhouse, he raced to the scene.

When later questioned about the guardhouse faux pas, Inspector Graham stated, "About 9:40 pm, Warrant Officer Truscott met me in the passage way outside the office in which Steven was seated with Trumbley. The father asked me in a belligerent manner how and where Steve had been picked up."

It's unclear if Daniel Truscott was indeed in a fighting mood or just simply deeply concerned with what was happening to his son. He fruitlessly tried to get the police to release Steven. Warrant Officer Truscott wanted to take the tired boy home and let the police resume their interrogation in the morning. The police refused to consider this request. Their interrogation of Truscott in the guardhouse resumed. Legally, Daniel Truscott could have removed his son from the guardhouse at any time. His son still wasn't under arrest which meant police couldn't hold him against his will. Only no one explained this to either father or son.

Other visitors arrived at the guardhouse throughout the evening, including Dr. David Brooks and a dazed Doris Truscott. Three policemen escorted Doris back to her home. She told the men they didn't need a search warrant if they wanted to look around. The Truscott's had nothing to hide. The police made a search and removed a pair of red jeans from a clothing line—the same jeans Truscott had worn June 9. His mother had dutifully washed the pants and was now drying them on the line. Dr. Brooks remained at the guardhouse.

Conversation at the guardhouse now began to revolve

around a medical examination. Daniel Truscott was asked if he would consent to his son being examined by a doctor. Warrant Officer Truscott initially refused, protesting that the police were railroading his son. In this tense atmosphere, Daniel Truscott turned to Sergeant Anderson, who was an acquaintance of his.

"(Truscott) asked Sgt. Anderson, 'What do you think, Charlie?' Sgt. Anderson said that in his opinion the boy should have a physical examination and that if no evidence was found it would be to his advantage. The father then consented and an examination was conducted in another office," declared Inspector Graham in his statement.

It was decided that Dr. Brooks shouldn't give the exam, because he was too involved with the case already to be unbiased. Daniel Truscott gave police the name of his family physician, Dr. John Addison, a General Practitioner in Clinton, ON. Dr. Addison was called and agreed to carry out the medical examination. He arrived at the guardhouse around 10:30 pm and was briefed on the situation by Dr. Brooks.

Dr. Addison asked Steven to strip naked then examined him, with the help of Dr. Brooks. It was the first time either physician had ever examined a rape suspect. There were a few bumps and scrapes but no major scars or scratches on Truscott's body. Dr. Addison did notice some small lesions on Steven's penis. The lesions were about the size of a quarter, on both sides of his penis. It looked like a friction burn. In the presence of his father, Truscott was asked if he'd been masturbating. Truscott admitted he had, but said his penis had been sore for four to five weeks.

The doctors concluded that the lesions were likely the result of rape, not self-pleasure. Once the physical exam was done, Dr. Addison decided to play detective. Around 1 am, he began peppering the very tired boy with questions. The doctor kept urging the boy to confess to the crime he was accused of. The boy refused.

In the early morning on July 13, Daniel Truscott was allowed to see his exhausted son again. Still protesting his innocence, Steven fell asleep on his father's shoulder. This was only a brief reprieve, however. The police had no intention of letting Daniel Truscott take his son home.

Over Daniel Truscott's protests, Steven was removed from the RCAF guardhouse by the OPP and taken back to Goderich. Inspector Graham believed the time had come to make an arrest.

"Steven Truscott was taken before Mrs. Mable Gray, Justice of the Peace, in Goderich and formally charged by Provincial Constable D.I. Trumbley at about 2:45 am, June 13th with the murder of Cheryl Lynne Harper ... he was remanded in custody to the Juvenile Detention room, court house, Goderich," wrote Corporal Sayeau, in his report.

After a few sleepless hours in the Juvenile Detention room, Truscott was taken before Juvenile Court Judge Dudley Holmes, in Goderich, Juvenile Court, for his arraignment. Then, the terrified boy was transferred to Huron County jail in Goderich. The jailhouse in question had been built in the 1840s and was made out of stone. It served as a prison right up the early 1970s. After it ceased to house prisoners, the jail was declared a national historic site by the Canadian government. It still stands today.

The boy's cell was tiny, with a steel-frame bed with a thin mattress and a chamber pot instead of a toilet. Truscott later recalled that he could raise his arms and touch both walls of his cell at the same time. It was a small relief when guards told Truscott had could use a toilet—based in an open corridor in the hallway and visible to staff and prisoners—rather than the chamber pot.

Truscott said later that he tried to remain calm and sane by focusing on childhood memories. By visualizing on better times, such as fishing with his beloved grandfather in British Columbia, the 14-year-old boy was able to keep from breaking down with fright and anguish.

Chapter Five: The Preliminary Hearing

The same day Steven Truscott was arraigned before Juvenile Court Judge Dudley Holmes, Lynne Harper was memorialized at a funeral. Funeral services were held at the Protestant chapel on the RCAF base. Some 30 Girl Guides in uniform served as honour guards for the body of the brutalized young girl. Harper herself was buried in a Girl Guide uniform. Sixteen airmen from the base acted as pallbearers. The Harper family was shattered in their grief.

Steven Truscott also faced the prospect of death. Judge Holmes had to decide whether to try the boy as an adult or a juvenile. At the time, judges could boost serious juvenile cases to adult court, if the juvenile was at least 14 years-old and trying them as an adult was in the community's best interest. This was no small matter; capital punishment was still in effect at the time for adult offenders (but not juveniles).

The Truscott family retained Frank Donnelly, Q.C., a well-known lawyer from Goderich, to take on their son's defence. Donnelly's first task was to try to keep the case tried in juvenile court. He reassured Daniel and Doris Truscott that their son would be vindicated in court. He told the traumatized parents that it was unlikely Steven would be convicted because of his youth, and the fact all the evidence against him was circumstantial.

If Daniel and Doris Truscott were reassured, their son wasn't.

"[Donnelly] had been introduced to my parents as one of Huron County's most prominent legal minds, a description that said little for the other lawyers of the area," Truscott told journalist Bill Trent, years later.

Truscott described his lawyer as a "balding man in his mid-fifties ... from the beginning, I had a child's instinctive distrust of him."

For their part, police continued interviewing children, even after Truscott had been arrested. The police set up a temporary interview station in the gym at A.V.M. Hugh Campbell School. Children were interviewed individually. Then their comments were transcribed into a typed statement which the children would were asked to sign.

Two of the children police were most interested in were Jocelyne Gaudet and Arnold George. Problem was, both kids seemed to have problems keeping their stories straight. Gaudet had initially told police she went searching for Lynne

Harper on the tractor trail into Lawson's Bush on the night of June 9. She soon changed her story and said she was looking for Truscott. She told police she also looked for Truscott on Bob Lawson's farm, arriving at 6:30 pm. Lawson, however, timed her arrival at 7:30 pm. Gaudet said she bumped into two people—Butch George and Philip Burns—when she emerged from the tractor trail.

George initially told police he saw Truscott and Harper bike by him on the bridge. Now he claimed he hadn't seen them at all. In post-arrest interviews, George said that he too had been looking for Truscott the night of June 9. A friend at the schoolyard told him Truscott had taken Harper on his bike down to the river. So George biked down to Lawson's Bush, where he said he encountered Gaudet, emerging from the woods.

"I asked her if she had seen Steve, she said 'no'. She asked me if I had seen Lynne. I said 'no'. Then I said, 'If I see Lynne I will tell you.' She said, '"OK,"' read a statement George gave police on June 15. George says he went swimming in the river then biked over to Truscott's home around 8:45 pm.

"Steve was in the house. He was wearing red pants and (a) white T-shirt when I arrived ... when I reached Steve's house I knocked and Steve came to the door. I said, 'Where have you been all the time?' and he said, 'Down the river'. I said, 'How come you rode Lynne down there' and he said, 'Oh, she wanted a lift down to the highway.' He mentioned about her getting a ride with a '59 Chev, yellow licence. I said, 'What was she doing along the bush with you' and he said, 'We were looking for a cow and calf, what do you want to know that for?' I said, 'Skip it. Let's play ball.' He said he had to babysit," George stated.

Police had less luck with Dougie Oates, who had been gathering turtles by the river. Oates claimed to have been within throwing distance of Harper and Truscott when they went by on the bridge. Oates refused to budge from this story. He also refused to sign a written statement police had typed up for him because his mother told him not to sign anything without one of his parents having a look first. In a similar fashion, Gord Logan continued to insist he saw Truscott and Harper on the bridge then saw Truscott return alone on his bike a few minutes later.

Another child, named Philip Burns, would prove more helpful to the police. Ten year old Philip said he was at the bridge around 7:00 pm on June 9. He told police he walked home, getting to the PMQs at the RCAF base at 7:30 pm. Along the way, he said he bumped into Gaudet and Butch George, but not Harper and Truscott. In other words, the two must have been somewhere else at the time.

The big issue in court was going to be, which witnesses would a jury believe?

Beyond finding enough witnesses to make their case, police and prosecutors faced two major problems. First, they had to establish that Truscott had enough time to commit the crime. It was estimated that Truscott left the school grounds around 7:25 pm then returned around 8 pm. Adding in travel time along the county road and into Lawson's Bush, this meant Truscott had barely ten minutes to assault and murder Harper.

On top of this very narrow window of opportunity, police

also had little in the way of physical evidence. Having failed to glean any fingerprints or hair samples from the crime scene that belonged to Truscott, police conducted a photo shoot to see if he was lying. They parked a 1959 Chevrolet at the intersection of Highway 8 and the county road. An officer standing on the bridge shot pictures of the vehicle, as other officers placed a series of coloured plates on the back of the car. They were trying to determine whether Truscott could indeed have spotted a yellow vehicle plate or sticker from his vantage point on the bridge.

On June 19, a young girl named Sandra Archibald went berry-picking on the edge of Lawson's Bush, near county road. While picking berries, Sandra came across Lynne Harper's RCAF locket. The locket in question was hanging on a barbed wire fence. Sandra took the locket home and showed her mother, who immediately contacted police. This could have been a big break, except that the place Sandra found the locket was 300 feet south of the tractor trail into Lawson's Bush. At the time, police were convinced Truscott had either lured or dragged Harper into the Bush via the tractor trail. Were her locket to fall off in the process, it surely would have ended up near the trail. The location of the locket presented a new dimension to the crime. Did the killer return to the death scene and deliberately place the locket in a place where someone could find it? Given that police had searched the area where Sandra found the locket only a day before and had uncovered nothing, this seemed like a reasonable assumption.

This evidence aside, authorities remained convinced that Truscott was guilty. Exceeding his duties as a physician once again, Dr. John Addison penned a damning letter to Inspector Harold Graham, dated June 22, 1959.

"Steve's explanation for the sore penis was not satisfactory in my opinion," wrote Dr. Addison. "He did not strike me as really understanding the seriousness of the charge laid against him. He did not protest strongly enough when I suggested he had molested Lynne. He agreed it could have happened. A normal boy accused of stealing cherries whether he were guilty or not would have vowed more vehemently that he was innocent."

"I cannot help but feel that this boy did not act to me like a normal boy while I was talking to him and examining him," continued the doctor. "He did not show enough resentment when I examined his body and asked him questions. Even the suggestion that he may have harmed Lynne brought no angry denial or an outbreak of tears ... I believe the possibility that this boy is mentally ill should be considered."

At the end of June, a decision was made regarding Truscott's status in court. It was decided he would be tried as an adult. He now faced the spectre of the death penalty. Defence lawyer Donnelly had lost this round. If he lost again at the criminal trial, there was a good chance his client might be executed.

Speaking to Trent, Steven Truscott complained bitterly of Donnelly's "ineptitude as a lawyer."

"I guess he tried hard enough, but in a completely lacklustre performance, he even lost the first skirmish in Juvenile Court," said Truscott, referring to Donnelly's losing battle to have him tried as a juvenile.

If crime historians are to be believed, citizens in Clinton felt a sense of relief now that Truscott was behind bars. The murdered girl was from an RCAF family, and the main suspect was also from an RCAF family. Like any community near a military facility, there was always a degree of animosity and suspicion between Clinton residents and RCAF base residents. Clintonites were greatly relieved that one of their own hadn't committed the crime.

"It is common knowledge that military or air force stations are not liked by civilians in the area. Clinton was no exception. An Air Force boy had killed an Air Force girl: let the Air Force look after its own: 'We don't want anything to do with them,'" author Isabel LeBourdais would write in her book, *The Trial of Steven Truscott*.

In July, the RCAF decided to transfer Daniel Truscott from Clinton to Ottawa. Warrant Officer Truscott was ordered to report in Ottawa on July 15. No reason was given for the transfer, though it seemed obvious the military wanted to remove the Truscott's from the Clinton base.

"Normally, a person on transfer was given two month's notice, but he was given a week! This meant he would have to travel 500 miles to visit me ... since there had been no mention of transfer prior to my arrest, it all seemed more than coincidental," Truscott later related to Trent.

As a result of the decision, the Truscott family now faced a long drive just to see their son. The Truscott's purchased a trailer and set it up in a park in Goderich. Daniel Truscott moved to Ottawa, as per the military's request, while the rest of his family set up quarters in the trailer. Every weekend,

Daniel journeyed to Goderich to join his family, and visit his son when he could.

In mid-July, Juvenile Court Judge Holmes—the same justice who had arraigned Truscott a month before—presided over a preliminary hearing in the case. The purpose of the preliminary hearing was to determine if there was sufficient evidence to proceed with an actual trial.

Frank Donnelly did not introduce a defence at the preliminary hearing, preferring just to cross-examine prosecution witnesses. Donnelly wanted to find out as much information as possible about the Crown's case without revealing anything about his own case. Under the courtroom rules of the day, the prosecution was not obliged to disclose all their evidence with the defence.

Dr. John Penistan took the stand to report on his inspection of Harper in Lawson's Bush, and his subsequent funeral home autopsy. Interestingly, the doctor deviated from his original time of death estimate. He testified that, based on his analysis of Harper's rigor mortis and the degree of putrefaction in her corpse, she could have died up to two and a half days prior to the autopsy. Not that this broadened time frame exonerated Truscott, the doctor was quick to add. He insisted that a closer examination of Harper's stomach contents indicated she had actually died within a couple hours of eating.

Dr. Brooks and Dr. Addison gave testimony about the state of Steven Truscott's penis. To Donnelly's questioning, Dr. Addison admitted that the sores on Truscott's penis might have been caused by masturbation, or putting his penis in a knothole.

Corporal John Erskine admitted on the stand that he wasn't able to retrieve any complete footprints from the crime scene, because the ground was too dry. Constable Donald Hobbs said Truscott had been polite and cooperative when he interviewed him, and didn't appear to have any visible scratches on his face or anywhere else. This was an important fact, given speculation that Harper had struggled with her assailant.

Biologist John Funk, from the Ontario attorney-general's laboratory, stated that he hadn't finished his analysis of Harper's stomach contents and therefore couldn't offer an opinion regarding her time of death. It was a jarring admission, given that Inspector Graham claimed he received an oral report indicating that lab tests have verified Dr. Penistan's time of death estimate. Funk in fact wouldn't file his report until late summer. In this manner, he was simply being cautious and meticulous. When he finally got around to filing his report, it didn't contain any speculation about time of death—something notoriously difficult to pin down through mere stomach content analysis.

Amazingly, such scientific haziness and false assumptions by police were largely overlooked at both the preliminary hearing and forthcoming criminal trial.

Arnold George's testimony was confusing and contradictory. He even managed to stumble over swearing his oath, offering a vague response when the judge asked him about the importance of telling the truth. On the stand, George admitted the he had changed his story to police, claiming first that he saw Truscott and Harper biking along the bridge over the Bayfield River, then saying he hadn't seen the two.

During his testimony, George recalled his alleged conversation with Truscott the night Harper disappeared. George said Truscott told him he had taken Harper into Lawson's Bush to look at a cow and her calf. In interviews with police, Truscott denied this conversation took place.

In later comments to Trent, Truscott noted his "shock and outrage" at "Butch's perfidy" and the ease with which his former friend lied to police.

The Crown made no attempt to explain how Truscott could have dragged Harper into Lawson's Bush (with his bicycle in tow, no less), raped and killed her, then gone back to see his friends in such a short time period. Nor was there any evidence entered as to why so little blood was found on the ground at the death scene (this seemed to indicate Harper was already dead or dying when she was dumped in Lawson's Bush).

Most importantly, no evidence was entered as to how a perfectly average 14 year-old boy somehow turned into a sociopathic sex-murderer, without getting any blood on himself, much less, sweat. The Crown chose also not to speculate on the peculiar, fetishistic elements of the crime, such as Harper's neatly rolled up socks and zippered shorts and the three tree branches arrayed over her corpse. To contemporary minds, these strange elements pointed to a mentally-disturbed sex offender. Sexual deviancy and psychology in general were not well understood at the time, however, and the Crown chose to ignore such vital clues. As it was, Judge Holmes decided that evidence was sufficient to proceed with a trial. Steven Truscott would be tried for the murder of Lynne Harper.

Chapter Six: The Trial and Conviction of Steven Truscott

On September 16, 1959, Steven Truscott's criminal trial began in Goderich, ON. Truscott sat in a prisoner's box facing Judge Robert Ferguson. He was in a daze much of the time, completely bewildered by dense technical debates about points of law and unable to comprehend how he ended up on trial for his life. Later, Truscott would speak of losing track of time during his trial. He retained his steely composure, however, which some jurors interpreted as a sign of a remorseless nature. In reality, a very scared 14 year-old boy was taken back to his tiny cell each night after the court proceedings were through.

Today we know about Post-traumatic Stress Disorder (PTSD)—a lingering psychological condition that strikes after a person undergoes an extreme trauma. Symptoms range from anxiety and anger to depression and numbed emotions. The disorder is very common among soldiers who've been in combat. Truscott was too young to join the army, but old enough to be tried and hanged by the state, an excruciating trauma made worse by being labelled a sex-murderer. While he wasn't diagnosed at the time, it's entirely possible Truscott suffered from PTSD during the trial.

Justice Ferguson imposed a publication ban on the proceedings of the trial, which meant journalists couldn't report on daily events inside the courthouse. The judge based his decision on Criminal Code strictures against publicity at trials involving defendants under sixteen. The end-result was a lack of investigative reporting on the case for the duration of the trial.

Dan Truscott sat with defence attorney Frank Donnelly at the lawyer's table, which was set in front of the prisoner's box. A second lawyer, named Dan Murphy, had been retained by Donnelly to help him with the trial. Donnelly himself was supremely confident, given that all the evidence against his client was circumstantial.

Doris Truscott sat in the public gallery. She could be near her son but was not allowed to touch him or speak with him. Doris had suggested putting a few women on the jury, preferably ones with sons the same age as Steven. Donnelly rejected this suggestion. He believed females were too emotional to serve on a jury. In the end, Donnelly and Crown Prosecutor Glenn Hays settled on 12 men for the jury. The 12 jurors were primarily farmers. The rest worked as labourers or merchants. There was also a barber and a milkman among the jury.

Truscott pled not guilty, and the trial proper got underway.

Shirley Harper was one of the first witnesses for the prosecution. Testifying on September 17, 1959, she insisted all was fine in the Harper household the night her daughter vanished. Mrs. Harper also testified that, as far as she knew, her daughter never hitch-hiked. This was misleading at best. Both Leslie Harper and the police initially speculated that Lynne had hitch-hiked to her grandmother's house the night she disappeared. Donnelly was unaware of these comments, as he lacked access to all the prosecution's files, making it difficult for him to challenge Shirley Harper's veracity.

Dr. John Penistan testified that Harper was strangled (with her own blouse) and once more confidently placed her time of death between 7:15 – 7:45 pm on June 9, based on stomach content analysis. The doctor acknowledged that other tests, such as studying the degree of putrefaction in Harper's corpse, pointed to a much broader time of death estimate. Crown Prosecutor Hays avoided any detailed discussion of this point, however.

Dr. Penistan said in his view, "death took place where the body was found" and that Harper's vaginal injuries "might possibly have been produced by a blind, violent thrust of the male organ."

When questioned by Donnelly, Dr. Penistan conceded that it was difficult to precisely judge time of death through medical tests. This was a major concession but Donnelly unfortunately didn't drive the point home for the benefit of the jury. Nor did Donnelly remind the doctor about his testimony at the preliminary hearing, in which he stated that Harper might have been murdered anywhere up to two-and-a-half days before her autopsy.

Doctors John Addison and David Brooks also offered seemingly damning medical testimony.

Their testimony did not come without controversy. Judge Ferguson was not impressed with Dr. Addison's interrogation of Truscott at the RCAF guardhouse. "You took on the role of a detective," rebuked the judge. Judge Ferguson ruled that the two doctors could testify about their medical findings, but not about any statements Truscott might have made during the examination.

For much of their time on the stand, the two doctors focused on the condition of Truscott's penis. Dr. Addison described two "raw" and "oozing" sores, about the size of a quarter, on both sides of Truscott's penis.

Asked what could have caused these injuries, and Dr. Addison said, "There would have to be friction in an oval shaped orifice ... something of an oval shape and sufficiently rough to cause a friction or wear of the outer surface of the skin."

The doctor did concede that the oval shaped orifice could have been a knothole, rather than Lynne Harper's genitals.

Dr. Brooks was considerably more explicit. He said Harper's vaginal injuries were the result of "a very inexpert attempt at penetration."

On the stand, Flying Officer Glen Sage—who had been in charge of the section of RCAF personnel who discovered Harper's body—said he found a footprint at the crime scene. The footprint had a wavy pattern and came from a shoe with a crepe rubber sole, he claimed. This was an odd piece of evidence given that the OPP's own identification officer, John

Erskine, had been unable to detect any clear footprints near Harper's body. Erskine wouldn't vouch for Sage's remarks. When called to testify, Erskine referred only to "scuff marks" around Harper, not footprints.

The Crown also placed emphasis on bicycle tire tracks found in Lawson's Bush, tracks allegedly similar to the bike Truscott was using on June 9. Once again, Erskine cast doubt on the evidence. He said he wasn't able to match the tracks to the racing bike Truscott had been riding. Under cross-examination from Donnelly, Erskine acknowledged that the bike tracks were probably made when the ground was wet. The area where the tracks were found, however, hadn't received any rain in weeks. In other words, any tracks found at the scene couldn't have been made by Truscott the night Harper disappeared, said Donnelly. While Erskine agreed with this conclusion, Donnelly failed to underline the importance of this concession to the jury.

Inspector Harold Graham's appearance in court on September 18, 1959, sparked a legal row between the lawyers regarding the validity of any statements Truscott had made to Graham during his interrogation. Judge Ferguson sent the jury out of the room as Donnelly and Hays debated. Donnelly demanded to know why his client wasn't given a warning about making statements that could later be used against him. On this issue, the judge sided with defence.

"There was no equality between this 14 year-old boy and a group of police officers who were examining him," noted Judge Ferguson.

As a young boy without an adult guardian present, Truscott couldn't have been expected to know what his legal rights were. While police were within the law to interview Truscott alone and not bother to inform him he was a key suspect on the verge of being arrested, doing so was less than ethical. Truscott's extended interrogation pitted seasoned policemen against an exhausted juvenile—hardly a fair match, noted the judge.

Truscott's statement to police was declared inadmissible. While this was a considerable victory for the defence, Donnelly hesitated to follow it up. Once the statement issue had been taken care of, Donnelly had few questions for the senior police officer. He didn't scrutinize Graham about the ethically dubious interrogation of his client.

Other police testimony was designed to impugn Truscott's honesty. Police officers said they stood at the bridge over the Bayfield River and tried unsuccessfully to read the licence plate numbers of cars speeding by on Highway 8. This was confusing, given that Truscott never claimed to have read any licence numbers, but rather, that he had spotted something yellow or orange at the back of the car that allegedly picked up Harper.

Police did concede that Truscott had been helpful and polite during interrogations, and consistently denied killing Harper.

Jocelyne Gaudet testified that Truscott had come to her house a little before 6:00 pm the night Harper disappeared. She said Truscott had made a date with her to see some newborn calves on Bob Lawson's farm. Gaudet claimed she biked to Lawson's farm after finishing her dinner and looked for Truscott but couldn't find him. When Donnelly questioned her, Gaudet admitted her memory was a bit shaky and that three weeks prior to Harper's murder, she had asked another boy (Gary Gilkes) to check out some calves at Lawson's farm with her.

On September 19, 1959, Arnold "Butch" George took the stand. During his confusing testimony, George claimed Truscott visited him at 6:00 pm the day after Harper disappeared. According to George, Truscott was in a bit of a jam. Truscott had given George's name to police as an alibi witness—someone who was near the Bayfield River and saw him bike by on the bridge with Harper the night of June 9. Only Truscott had made a mistake: George really hadn't been at the river. Truscott had mistaken him for Gordon Logan. Truscott wanted George to lie, and tell police he really had been at the river and could vouch for his alibi. While George's testimony was somewhat garbled, it was potentially devastating. His testimony presented Truscott as a duplicitous liar with something to hide.

On September 25, 1959, the defence began its case. Donnelly was already at a huge disadvantage. He had only a fraction of the resources available to the prosecution and wasn't allowed to question his own witnesses about statements they made to police, even when those statements put Truscott in the clear. Under courtroom rules of the day, the statements to police were considered the property of the Crown. Donnelly could only use them if the Crown Prosecutor gave his permission, which was not forthcoming. Donnelly was also unable to access a wealth of notes, bulletins and reports from police and other officials that would have strengthened his case.

Donnelly's first witness was a meteorology instructor from RCAF station Clinton, who testified about the lack of rain prior to Harper's murder. This testimony was designed to cast doubt on the relevance of bicycle tire tracks found on the tractor trail. If there had been no rain in the area for some time then clearly the tracks had been made well before June 9.

Next to testify was Dr. Berkely Brown, who had served as a medic in the Canadian Army in Europe during the Second World War. Dr. Brown had examined thousands of soldiers, including men accused of rape. He cast doubt on the theory that Truscott's penile lesions were the result of forced intercourse on a young virgin.

"I would think that it would be highly unlikely that penetration would produce a lesion of this sort. It is interesting that the penis is rarely injured in rape, to begin with. When it is injured, it is usually a tearing injury confined to the head of the penis," stated Dr. Brown.

Dr. Brown also testified that the stomach of a 12 year-old girl normally took three and a half to four hours to empty, not two hours as Dr. Penistan had stated. Factors, such as stress and terror could also impact digestion time, added Dr. Brown.

On September 26, 1959, it was Doris Truscott's turn to testify. She told the court that Steven had left the house after dinner to meander before his 8:30 pm babysitting duties. During cross-examination, Prosecutor Hays tried to make Doris Truscott out to be a co-conspirator with her son, washing his pants to cover up valuable evidence.

Dougie Oates testified he was within a few feet of Truscott and Harper when they passed by him on the bridge, heading to the highway. Dougie stated he had left the bridge around 7:30 pm. Hays asked repeatedly whether the boy could have been mistaken, that he might have seen Truscott at 6:30 pm, not after 7 pm as he kept insisting.

Gordon Logan provided one of the most important defence testimonies. He repeated what he had told police; that he'd been swimming in the river on June 9, then climbed out. Perched on a rock, he looked toward the bridge and saw Harper and Truscott cross together. A few minutes later, he saw Truscott return, alone.

Truscott himself did not testify, on the advice of his lawyer. Author Isabel LeBourdais suggests Donnelly was concerned how the 14 year-old boy would fare on the stand. While Truscott had remained remarkably well-composed throughout most of the trial, it was unclear if he could endure the vicious cross-examination sure to follow his testimony. Cross examination would have been a humiliating experience, complete with questions about his masturbatory habits, genital sores and personal cleanliness—topics young teenagers are loathe to discuss among themselves much less in a courtroom. On the other hand, putting Truscott on the stand might have made the boy seem more sympathetic to the jury.

A total of 74 witnesses took the stand over 11 days of testimony. Some 77 exhibits were displayed during the trial and the court reporter recorded between 350,000 – 400,000 words. Not a single witness claimed to have seen Truscott take Harper into Lawson's Bush. Nor was there any physical evidence tying Truscott to the crime. The prosecution's case was entirely based on circumstantial evidence.

Certain witnesses from the preliminary hearing were not asked to testify at the trial. They included John Funk and Dr. Noble

Sharpe, from the Ontario attorney-general's lab. Funk had written a brief (one page) report on Lynne Harper's stomach contents, but it wasn't very helpful for the prosecution. The doctor merely listed the contents of Harper's stomach and made no attempt to guess time of death. Donnelly, of course, had no idea this damning report even existed.

After both sides presented their case, Judge Ferguson only gave the lawyers a few hours to put together their summations. This fit a pattern of the lightning pace of the entire Truscott saga. Truscott had been arrested within one day of the discovery of Harper's body then tried three months later—a startlingly fast chain of events by modern standards.

On September 29, 1959, Donnelly made his final address to the jury.

"There is no direct evidence which in any way links this boy with that murder," Donnelly told the jury.

Then, point by point, the defence lawyer dismissed the prosecution's case. Donnelly said bicycle tire marks found at the crime scene were clearly old. He said George and Gaudet weren't reliable witnesses, discredited Dr. Penistan's autopsy results and stated that Truscott's penis lesions were probably caused by masturbation.

"There is some evidence that the girl was not killed in this bush," said Donnelly. He also pointed out that had Truscott committed the crime, he surely would have been covered in blood and been in a frenzied state when he biked back to the school grounds. Yet none of the witnesses who chatted with Truscott after he returned from biking Harper down the county road reported seeing anything unusual about the boy.

During his final address, Crown Prosecutor Hays implied that a "footprint" found at the crime scene matched Truscott's shoes and said no blood was found on the boy's clothes because he had taken them off before assaulting Harper. Truscott carefully cleaned his body after the crime and had his mother wash his jeans, to eliminate evidence, added Hays.

The Crown also theorized that Gaudet had been Truscott's intended target.

"He called [on Gaudet] at ten to six but she was having her supper, and I suggest to you, gentleman, that if they were late having their supper, it was God's blessing to that girl! I suggest he saw a substitute in Lynne Harper ... she went with him to the bush and to her doom!" exclaimed Hays.

Hays admitted George had lied when he told initially police he had seen Harper and Truscott together on the bridge.

"But when Lynne's body was found, [George] came to a realization that to protect a friend can just go so far, and then he gave a right statement," explained Hays.

While urging the jury to accept George's testimony, Hays told them to disregard the testimony of Oates and Logan.

One thing Hays did not attempt to do in his final address was to reconstruct the actual crime, and explain how Truscott might have actually gone about raping and killing his classmate.

Once Hays finished, Judge Ferguson instructed the jury to start considering their verdict that very same evening. The justice gave the jury a 10 minute break then offered his summation of the case.

During his summation, Judge Ferguson mistakenly said that Truscott claimed to have read licence plate numbers from the bridge, which he never did. The judge questioned whether the children on the school grounds who saw Truscott at 8:00 pm or so could have seen him clearly, given the late hour. In fact, the sun was still up when Truscott biked back to the school grounds. The judge also suggested that Truscott might have taken Harper out to Highway 8 only to bring her back to Lawson's Bush where he killed her.

The jury was sent out of the courtroom five times while Donnelly challenged various aspects of the judge's summation. While he was doing his job, Donnelly's constant objections didn't endear him to the jury.

At 10:55 pm on September 30, 1959, after deliberating for only a few hours, the jury returned with a verdict: guilty, with a plea for mercy. Doris Truscott began to cry while Steven Truscott turned white. For the first time at the trial, Steven could been seen tearing up.

As it turned out, Truscott had good reason to cry. Judge Ferguson ignored the jury's recommendation of mercy and handed out the harshest punishment under the law.

"Steven Murray Truscott, I have no alternative but to pass the following sentence upon you," said the judge. "The jury have found you guilty after a fair trial. The sentence of this court upon you is that you be taken from here [to the Huron County jail] ... and there be kept in close confinement until Tuesday, the 8th day of December, 1959, and upon that day and date you will be taken to the place of execution and that you there be hanged by the neck *until you are dead* and may the Lord have mercy on your soul. Remove the prisoner."

Chapter Seven: Life Behind Bars

On October 5, 1959, Pierre Berton, then a scrappy columnist with *The Toronto Star*, wrote a poem about Steven Truscott. The poem did not mention Truscott by name, or even claim he was innocent. Entitled, *Requiem for a Fourteen Year-Old*, Berton's work simply suggested it was immoral to hang such a young boy.

The poem, in part read:

> "In Goderich town
> The Sun abates
> December is coming
> And everyone waits;
> In a small, dark room
> On a small, hard bed
> Lies a small, pale boy
> Who is not quite dead.
> The cell is lonely

The cell is cold
October is young
But the boy is old;
Too old to cringe
And too old to cry
Though young—
But never too young to die."
"In Goderich town
The trees turn red
The limbs go bare
As their leaves are bled
And the days tick by
As the sky turns lead
For the small, scared boy
On the small, stark bed
A fourteen-year old
Who is not quite dead."

For his poignant poem, Berton received reams of hate mail. Readers were outraged that he had expressed sympathy for a convicted killer, albeit, a youthful one. Some readers went so far as to suggest Berton's daughters deserved to be raped, because of the opinions he expressed.

Frank Donnelly tried to reassure Dan and Doris Truscott that their son's sentence would likely be commuted to life imprisonment. Not that Donnelly was around much to provide personal reassurances; two days after Truscott was convicted, Donnelly became a judge on the Superior Court of Ontario. It was a promotion he was supposed to get at the start of the summer, but had to temporary put aside for the sake of the Truscott trial.

The vehemence that greeted Pierre Berton's poem was indicative of the intense emotions stirred up by the trial.

While many Canadians were appalled that a 14 year-old could be sentenced to death on shaky circumstantial evidence, others were convinced justice had been served. This was partly a reflection of the times. Back in the late 1950s, it was generally assumed that if a person had their day in court and was convicted, they were undoubtedly guilty. The notion that police and courts could make a mistake was unthinkable.

The small-town environment in which the crime and trial took place might have also influenced events.

"Over the years, writers and commentators have observed that had I gone on trial in Toronto, or any large Canadian city, it is almost a foregone conclusion that I would been acquitted. I could feel the antipathy of that small-town jury, moved not by sympathy for Lynne but hatred for me," Truscott would later tell journalist Bill Trent.

If he was hurt by his friend Arnold George's testimony, Truscott was infuriated by Prosecutor Glenn Hays' treatment of his mother. "I wanted nothing so much in the world at that particular moment as to leave the prisoner`s box and take a swing at the arrogant Mr. Glenn Hays Q.C.," recalled Truscott, years later.

Truscott continued his grim existence in what he would later call the "Goderich dungeon". At one point, he woke up to the sounds of hammering outside the Huron County jail. Sick with anxiety, Truscott thought at first his jailers were building a scaffold from which he would hang. It turned out jail staff were doing some unrelated repair work. While relieved, Truscott remained on death row. He was kept in his cell almost 24 hours a day, let out only to bathe. He even spent

December 25, 1959 in lock-up—"the first of ten Christmases I was to spend behind bars," he later noted gloomily.

Since Donnelly was now occupied with other tasks, the Truscott family hired a lawyer named John O'Driscoll to handle an appeal. O'Driscoll submitted his appeal on October 10, 1959. He appealed the verdict on the grounds that the judge's comments to the jury were biased and that the jury's decision was "contrary to the weight of evidence."

On January 12, 1960, five judges on the Ontario Court of Appeal spent three days reviewing the Truscott case. To accommodate the Court of Appeal, Truscott's execution date was rescheduled for mid-February.

The court refused to hear new evidence. Truscott's lawyers could only fight on points of law. O'Driscoll argued that Justice Robert Ferguson was biased towards the prosecution. While the judges criticized the police for their tactics in the Truscott case, they dismissed his appeal. The decision came down January 20, 1960, two days after Truscott's birthday. He was now 15.

Within hours of losing his appeal, Truscott sentence was commuted to life imprisonment by the federal government. It was decided to send Truscott to the Ontario Training School for Boys, a facility for juvenile offenders in Guelph, ON, until he turned 18, at which point he would be transferred to a federal prison in Kingston, ON.

In February, O'Driscoll tried to appeal Truscott's case to the Supreme Court of Canada. The Supreme Court, however, wasn't interested in hearing the case. That same month, Truscott was slapped in leg irons and handcuffs and removed from Huron County jail. To satisfy the letter of the law (which stated Truscott had to be held in a federal prison), authorities took Truscott to the Kingston Penitentiary for a single night. Along the way, police stopped for lunch at a restaurant. They escorted Truscott, handcuffs, leg-irons and all, inside. Being handcuffed, Truscott had to rely on a kind waitress to cut his steak for him. He ate his dinner while everyone in the restaurant gawked at the boy in cuffs. After that, Truscott spent a single night in the Kingston Penitentiary. Next day, he was put back in chains and sent to Guelph.

The Ontario Training School aimed to be rehabilitative, not punitive. Guards didn't wear police-style uniforms, but rather, green jackets, white shirts and grey dress pants. The boys at the school wore black boots, khaki pants and T-shirts. There were three shops at the facility, where boys could learn machining, carpentry or sheet metal skills. Truscott opted for machine shop.

"We were awakened at 7:30 am, did calisthenics, ate breakfast and went to the shops assigned us. Our work day ended at 4:00 pm and after supper we could read or play cards until 10:00 pm. There was an active sports program on weekends. In winter we played basketball, hockey and broom ball. The summer sports included softball, football and soccer," Truscott told journalist Trent.

The Training School was a considerable improvement over the Goderich jail. It was set in a rural locale, which pleased Truscott, ever the outdoorsman. Most of the staff behaved decently to Truscott and he didn't have to greet visitors from behind a metal screen, as he did in Goderich. At the Training School, inmates met family members face-to-face in a visiting room. The centre remained a place of confinement and submission, however. Some guards enjoyed baiting the more high-strung prisoners, getting them to act out then slapping them with disciplinary penalties, like loss of television viewing privileges.

Years later, Truscott recalled the intense loneliness he felt at the Ontario Training School. While he enjoyed visits from his family, these encounters left him feeling depressed for hours after they were over. He continued to maintain a placid facade, however, making a personal pledge never to break down in tears.

By all standards, Truscott was an exemplary prisoner. He enjoyed carpentry and doing woodwork. Truscott also gained a reputation as a skilled athlete and was generally left alone by Training School bullies.

By this point, both of Truscott's parents were living on an air base near Ottawa. Every month, Doris Truscott made the gruelling journey to see her son in Guelph. She worked in a bakery, grocery store and cafeteria to pay for gas. Dan Truscott also took a second job, working part-time some nights at a racetrack.

In the early 1960s, Truscott acquired a new defender. Her name was Isabel LeBourdais, and she was a stay-at-home mother in Toronto who was married to a writer. LeBourdais was also a writer, with publishing credits in high-profile magazines such as *Chatelaine* and *Saturday Night*. She was also active in the fight for civil rights for minorities and psychiatric patients.

Shocked by Truscott's death sentence, LeBourdais began to

investigate his case. She obtained the court transcripts of the trial and became the first objective outsider to examine the facts in detail. On April 22, 1960, LeBourdais penned a letter to Doris and Dan Truscott. She introduced herself and said she wanted to write a magazine article about their son. She met with the Truscott parents then journeyed to Clinton for a first-hand look at the Harper crime scene. LeBourdais also did extensive interviews, with lawyers from the case and 11 of the jurors.

Through her research, LeBourdais concluded that Truscott was innocent. In her opinion, authorities didn't consider important evidence that pointed to other suspects. LeBourdais discovered that jurors completely bought Dr. Penistan's contentious time-of-death estimate. Other jurors were convinced that Truscott had left clear footprints at the scene of the crime. The boy's outwardly calm manner in court was seen as lack of remorse.

"I knew the boy was guilty right from the start but he was so young and it was so sad, and I kept hoping that somehow they would prove he didn't do it, but they couldn't because of course he did," said one juror, according to LeBourdais.

Another juror said he voted guilty because Truscott "told such awful lies about seeing the licence plate numbers from the bridge. There was his footprint right there beside the body!"

When magazine editors balked at accepting an article on the Truscott case, LeBourdais decided to expand her investigation and write a book. Maybe a book would stand a better chance of getting published.

In late 1961, LeBourdais inked a contract with McClelland and Stewart. The publisher, however, became concerned about the explosive nature of her expose, and ended up rejecting the manuscript when it was submitted in late 1962. LeBourdais took the rejection in stride and continued her investigation while looking for a new publisher.

Truscott's 18th birthday, on January 18, 1963, was a bitter occasion. Now that he was an adult, authorities moved him to Collins Bay Penitentiary in Kingston, ON.

In interviews with Trent, Truscott described the penitentiary as "a huge, dismal place of gray Kingston limestone with a stone wall 20 feet high." Truscott was placed in cellblock C, cell number five. He was given prison clothes (black boots, grey pants, white T-shirt) and a number, 6730.

Truscott's cell was four feet wide, eight feet high and seven feet long. It contained a fold-up bed, a toilet, sink and small cupboard. The small, barred window in the cell looked out onto the prison yard which was almost permanently shaded by the huge stone walls of the institution.

Collins Bay prison boasted a machine shop run by a tough but kindly staffer named Joe Fowler. The machine shop looked after all farm and kitchen equipment in the facility, and only trusted prisoners could work there. With his experience from Guelph and his responsible demeanour, Truscott soon became a machine shop regular.

Once more, Truscott got along well with the prisoners and staff. One aspect of life at Collins Bay he didn't appreciate was the constant probing by prison psychiatrists. The latter repeatedly tried to examine his psyche in an attempt to get him to admit to murdering Harper. Among other drugs, Truscott was given LSD and sodium pentothal (the so-called "truth serum") in an effort to loosen his tongue. It didn't work. Truscott refused to admit guilt.

Truscott quietly served his sentence and in early August, 1964, applied for parole. The wording on his parole application would later come to cause him considerable grief.

"All I ask is just one chance to prove that I am worthy of being allowed to mix with society. I am working very hard at my trade and have learned quite a bit. I have done my best to keep a clean record while I am serving my sentence ... I have paid five years of my life but this has taught me that crime does not pay, so all I ask is, please grant me one chance to make a success of my life and prove that one dreadful mistake does not mean that I will ever make another one," Truscott wrote.

Truscott later explained that he never meant to imply that his "one dreadful mistake" was Harper's murder. W.J. Haggerty, the classification officer assigned to Truscott in Kingston, added a few comments to the parole application that made this clear. "Truscott still claims innocence of the present offence but accepts his sentence with the feeling that nothing can be done now," wrote Haggerty.

Truscott's parole application was turned down, and life continued to grind on in Collins Bay. As his time behind bars increased, Truscott admitted he felt increasingly distant from his family.

In January 1966, Isabel LeBourdais' explosive book, *The Trial of Steven Truscott*, was finally published—in Great Britain. Every major publisher in Canada had turned the book down.

Only after the book came out in the UK did McClelland and Stewart pick it up in Canada, releasing a Canadian version in March, 1966.

The Trial of Steven Truscott was shocking, and not just because it suggested the man at the centre of the book was innocent. Some people were outraged that a writer—much less a female writer—dared to suggest police and courts were not infallible. The book sold 60,000 copies in a few weeks and prompted prominent Canadians to take an interest in the case.

On March 18, 1966, John Diefenbaker, former Prime Minister turned Opposition Leader, stood in the House of Commons to deliver a broadside.

"...because of the revelations made in a book by Mrs. LeBourdais, which is about Steven Truscott's trial and the circumstances surrounding it, in the interests of justice ... would the Prime Minister give consideration to an investigation into this matter, by way of royal commission or otherwise, to ascertain the true facts?" demanded Diefenbaker.

In response, Prime Minister Lester Pearson said he had discussed Truscott's situation with the Solicitor General who was looking into the case.

The Trial of Steven Truscott was quickly banned at Collins Bay. Truscott received a smuggled copy from a sympathetic guard, whose lawn mower he had fixed.

"[The book] brought home to me once more what a tragic farce the trial had been and how prejudiced the people of

Huron County had been at the time. I had considered the people of Clinton and Goderich little better than a lynch mob but Isabel LeBourdais' book drove the point home again. It made me realize that there would never be any place on earth I would despise with the same intensity that I loathed the communities of Clinton and Goderich," Truscott later told Trent.

Needless to say, authorities were outraged by the book. Harold Graham, now an assistant commissioner for the OPP (he would eventually serve as OPP commissioner, from 1973 - 1981) met with officials, including Hank Sayeau and members of the Justice Department to discuss *The Trial of Steven Truscott*. Like Graham, Sayeau had risen in the police hierarchy, to the rank of inspector.

"It was agreed by both the federal and provincial governments, that there should be a rebuttal to the book," wrote Assistant Commissioner Graham in an April 4, 1966 memo.

Graham went on to suggest a royal commission be established—not to investigate the Truscott case, but to bad-mouth LeBourdais. The former Inspector also kicked around the idea of having the Minister of Justice or Solicitor General denounce the book in the House of Commons.

On April 19, 1966, Solicitor General Larry Pennell announced to the House of Commons that the Truscott case would be reviewed. One week later, Ottawa said they would refer the case to the Supreme Court of Canada for a historic rehearing.

"There exists widespread concern as to whether there was a miscarriage of justice in the conviction of Steven Murray Truscott and it is in the public interest that the matter be inquired into," read the blandly worded April 27, 1966 Order-in-Council that referred the most notorious murder case in Canadian history to the top court in the land.

Chapter Eight: The Supreme Court of Canada

As the Supreme Court prepared to review Steven Truscott's conviction, Dr. John Penistan finally got around to writing up his autopsy findings from the Harper case. He hoped to submit his autopsy report to a medical journal for publication. Dr. Penistan sent a draft copy of his report to OPP Assistant Commissioner Harold Graham, along with a letter dated May 19, 1966.

"I do not believe I have changed any of my essential conclusions as a result of my review (one is tempted to refer to it as an 'agonizing reappraisal' in the current jargon: the adjective is probably better justified here than in most cases)," wrote Dr. Penistan.

Following this somewhat confusing statement, the doctor went on to attack his own findings. He declared that his estimate of Harper's time of death could only be used to exclude suspects, not point the finger of guilt at anyone (a rather disingenuous argument to say the least). Dr. Penistan also hedged his bets about the nature of Harper's injuries.

"The evident injuries to the genitals ... could have been inflicted with a blunt instrument, such as a broomstick. Absolute proof of coitus by way of demonstrable spermatozoa in the vagina was lacking," wrote the doctor.

This was a far cry from his court testimony in which he said her injuries were caused by "a blind furious thrust of a male organ."

More significantly, the doctor cast doubt on his initial estimate of Harper's time of death.

"All findings are compatible with death within two hours of Lynne's last meal. However, the degree of rigor and decomposition are compatible also with death at a later time ... the state of the stomach content is also compatible with death at a later time, provided that digestion and emptying were delayed by some physical or psychological episode occurring within approximately two hours of the last meal," wrote Dr. Penistan.

Graham reviewed the article and made it clear he didn't approve of publishing it without serious revisions. The original draft was never published.

Dr. Penistan had good reason to disavow his own findings: in a memo of his own to William Bowman, director of public prosecutions for Ontario, Dr. Noble Sharpe blasted the pathologist for not mentioning "the variables which affect stomach contents. This applies also to his evidence re rigor mortis and decomposition ... I also criticized him for using definite times in places of saying one or two hours—saying 7:15 to 7:45 seems so absolute!"

Doctor reports aside, police were picking up fresh tips and leads now that the Truscott case was back in the news.

In a June 15, 1966 memo, Graham cited "an aged couple named Mr. And Mrs. Fletcher Townsend of Clinton [who] had seen a young girl hitchhiking in the vicinity of Highway 8 and the county road the night that Lynne Harper disappeared."

Given that Truscott claimed he saw Harper hitch-hiking on the highway then getting into a car, this was a potentially important lead. The memo stated that the Townsend's had been interviewed June 11, 1959, by Constable Donald Trumbley in their Clinton, ON, home.

"After the discussion between Townsend and his wife, and the fact that both agreed it was near darkness [when the alleged sighting occurred], no further investigation was made. We were satisfied at the time it was an aged couple who were trying to be helpful in the investigation," wrote Graham.

Unfortunately for Truscott, none of this information— neither Dr. Penistan's draft copy, Graham's report, nor Dr. Sharpe's memo—was made available for Truscott's lawyers at the Supreme Court hearings.

On October 5, 1966, a two-week hearing on Truscott's trial opened before the Supreme Court of Canada. The historic review marked the first time the Supreme Court ever heard live witnesses. The young man at the center of the review was unnerved by his sudden exposure to the outside world. The drive from Collins Bay Penitentiary in Kingston, Ontario, to Ottawa was like a journey through an alien landscape. Truscott later recalled the strange sensation of seeing ordinary people carrying out their everyday business. Talking to someone other than a guard, prisoner, lawyer or family member was also an intense experience. In a restaurant (this time, without handcuffs on his wrists) a discomfited Truscott could barely respond when a waitress asked for his order.

Truscott was kept in a cell at the Carleton County Jail, "an old dungeon of a place" that reminded him of the prison in Goderich, he later commented. During the day, he was taken to the Supreme Court of Canada, for his historic review.

Before the Supreme Court, Truscott maintained his usual calm demeanour. Inside, he was edgy and jumping, fearful of the stares that greeted his presence. His fear of being at the centre of attention had become "a sort of phobia .... I imagined everyone was staring at me, a situation which persisted to a degree for some time after my release from prison," Truscott told Trent.

The Crown was represented at the review by William Bowman. Just like Glenn Hays before him, Bowman worked closely with police officials to prepare the Crown's case. Witnesses would be questioned for the prosecution by Donald Scott, a lawyer from Seaforth, ON.

Truscott was represented by Ted Joliffe (a personal friend of Isabel LeBourdais) and Arthur Martin, a well-respected criminal lawyer. Joliffe was a left-leaning progressive lawyer who had read LeBourdais manuscript and shared her belief in Truscott's innocence. Martin, meanwhile, was a powerhouse attorney hailed by *Maclean's* magazine in the 1950s for his ability to win acquittals for defendants accused of murder.

The first witnesses were Dr. Noble Sharpe and John Funk, the medical experts from the attorney-general's laboratory. On the stand, Funk refused to validate Dr. Penistan's opinion that Harper died between 7:15 – 7:45 pm on June 9, roughly two hours after eating. Dr. Sharpe took the same position. He testified that digestion can be impacted by intense emotion, including fear and anger.

Dr. Charles Sutherland Petty, assistant medical examiner for the state of Maryland, testified that stomach contents were not a "reliable guide" for estimating time of death and said Harper could have died "anywhere from minutes to hours" after her last meal.

Other medical experts focused on the state of Truscott's genitals.

Dr. Emilian Marcinkowsky, a physician at the Guelph Training School for Boys, testified that he had treated Truscott for dermatitis and "an inflamed cyst of the dorsum of the penis." His testimony was designed to give a boost to Truscott's contention that his lesions pre-dated Harper's disappearance.

Dr. Norman Wrong, a graduate lecturer at the University of Toronto and former president of the Canadian Dermatological Association, offered similar testimony. The doctor suggested Truscott's penile lesions might simply have been cold sores that became infected, perhaps by riding a bicycle while wearing denim pants.

"I do not recall ever seeing traumatic lesions on the shaft of the penis as a result of intercourse," added Dr. Wrong, who had served in the military and physically examined soldiers accused of rape.

Truscott's testimony on October 6, 1966, was the highlight of the Supreme Court hearing. Truscott unfortunately, did not make the most compelling witness (which might have been another reason he didn't testify at his original trial). Truscott stumbled over details, admitted to a bad memory and confessed he wasn't even sure how old his older brother Ken was.

Truscott said he had been at a party with Harper a few days before she disappeared, but denied having any romantic interest in the girl. Recounting his actions on the evening of June 9, Truscott repeated the same story he had given countless times to police. He told the court he had given Harper a lift on his bicycle to Highway 8 and dropped her off. Truscott had biked away, and watched as she got into a car.

Truscott testified that his penile lesions made their debut, "about six weeks before I was picked up. And it started off, what appeared to be little blisters and it continued to worsen from there until it was in the state it was when I was picked up ... one blister would break and it just seemed that more would appear." The young man said he was "too embarrassed" to tell his father about his condition.

Truscott was quizzed about his choice of words in his August, 1964 parole application. He insisted he didn't intend to make an admission of guilt.

Martin asked Truscott the ultimate question: "Did you kill Miss Harper?" Truscott said no.

Defence witness Dr. Francis Edward Camps testified after Truscott. A leading British authority on the medical aspects of criminal offences, Dr. Camps was director of the department of forensic medicine at the University of London medical school in the United Kingdom. He was so offended at what he considered the weak medical evidence used to convict Truscott he contacted Isabel LeBourdais' publisher in 1966, offering his services.

Testifying on October 11, 1966, Dr. Camps described Dr. Penistan's definitive 7:15 – 7:45 pm time frame as "dangerously misleading." He suggested the sexual assault on Harper probably didn't take place in Lawson's Bush, given the lack of semen found at the crime scene.

Some psychiatrists testified for the prosecution that Truscott was highly disturbed and sociopathic. Defence doctors said Truscott was perfectly normal and not suffering from any mental disorders.

Martin entered important technical information as evidence. Prior to the hearing, Martin hired private detectives to do tests from the bridge over the Bayfield River, to determine visual acuity. The detectives held up cards of different colours next to the rear bumper of a 1959 Chevrolet. People standing on the bridge easily identified the colours, he reported to the Supreme Court.

Once the witnesses had been heard, the lawyers submitted their written briefs and presented oral arguments.

Martin spoke for two and a half days, starting January 25, 1967 on why the justices should order a new trial. He highlighted the unreliability of witnesses such as Jocelyne

Gaudet and Arnold "Butch" George. Martin also pointed out the obvious: if Truscott really did have criminal designs on Harper, it's unlikely he would have left the school grounds with the girl in front of a host of witnesses.

Martin critiqued Dr. Penistan's autopsy findings and said the prosecution had been unable to prove that the lesions on Truscott's penis were the product of rape. Martin attacked footprint evidence used by the prosecution and told the court that Harper had debris under her fingernails, indicating she had fought with her assailant. Police were never able to find any of Harper's blood or hair on Truscott, much less unusual scars. The defence lawyer suggested Harper had been murdered elsewhere then dumped in Lawson's Bush by someone other than his client.

On January 27, 1967, Bowman summarized the prosecution's case. He urged the court to disregard any medical testimony about Harper's corpse that didn't come from Dr. Penistan or Dr. Brooks. These two men, after all, had performed the actual autopsy while other medical experts took their information from photographs and reports and was therefore unreliable. Bowman defended the police investigation of Truscott and his subsequent trial. He suggested that behind his seemingly calm facade, Truscott was really quite troubled.

The justices took these summations under consideration and spent months considering the case.

On May 4, 1967, the Supreme Court of Canada voted 8-1 to uphold Truscott's conviction.

"The effect of the additional evidence which was heard by this court, considered in its entirety, strengthens the view that the verdict of the jury ought not to be disturbed," read the decision. "There were many incredibilities inherent in the evidence given by Truscott before us and we do not believe his testimony."

In other words, the Supreme Court of Canada thought Truscott was a liar.

The justices might have also been influenced by another factor: four of the judges had been sitting in 1960, when the Supreme Court turned down Truscott's initial appeal. If these justices conceded that Truscott deserved a new trial, it would be an admission that their earlier decision was wrong.

Dan and Doris Truscott heard the news in a home in Toronto, with lawyer Joliffe and author Isabel LeBourdais by their sides. Truscott's mother tried to comfort her bitterly disappointed son over the telephone. LeBourdais also spoke to Truscott, promising not to give up the fight to clear his name. Daniel Truscott was too upset to speak over the phone.

The Truscott's were somewhat heartened by the fact Justice Emmett Hall disagreed with the ruling and offered a minority opinion

"There were grave errors in the trial ... having considered the case fully, I believe that the conviction should be squashed and a new trial directed. I take the view that the trial was not conducted according to law," wrote Judge Hall.

"I appreciate that after nearly eight years many difficulties will be met with if a new trial is held both on the part of the Crown and on the part of the accused, but these difficulties are relatively insignificant when compared to Truscott's fundamental right to be tried according to law ... a bad trial remains a bad trial. The only remedy for a bad trial is a new trial," the justice added.

Truscott didn't have long to brood. In the spring of 1967, he was hit with more devastating news. Malcolm Stienburg, a sympathetic prison chaplain at Collins Bay, took Truscott aside and told him his parents were splitting up. Truscott was greatly dismayed by his parent's breakup. Dan and Doris had been his rock, his solid link to the outside world.

While separated, Dan and Doris Truscott remained dedicated to Steven's case, as did LeBourdais. They were no longer alone in their struggle to prove Truscott's innocence. Unlike the late 1950s, the late 1960s was a rebellious time. Young people started questioning their elders on all matter of political, social, economic and cultural issues.

Among the nascent rebels of the era was a teenage girl named Marlene who lived in Guelph, ON. Her father was a union organizer and her family had a strong social conscience. She read about Truscott's case in *the Star Weekly* magazine and was appalled at the perceived injustice. Marlene, who was roughly the same age as Truscott, purchased LeBourdais' book and began clipping newspaper files on the case. She sent an upbeat poem to Dan and Doris Truscott and a letter to LeBourdais.

The 1967 Supreme Court decision against Truscott only cemented Marlene's resolve. She put together a petition for a new trial for Truscott and managed to gather 3,000 signatures.

In the spring of 1968, conditions improved greatly for Truscott at Collins Bay. He was transferred from the prison to the prison farm, which meant he could work outdoors. A self-professed country boy, Truscott loved the freedom of working outside. When he was done his labours, Truscott could fish in a creek that ran through the prison farm. He also discovered one of the farm fields abutted a drive-in movie theatre. At night, Truscott and other farm inmates took a tractor to the edge of this field and watched movies on the massive drive-in screen.

Truscott began taking a political science course with a professor from Queen's University who came to visit the prison farm annex. Truscott even received permission to take classes on the Queen's campus itself. He enjoyed classes in English and political science, but felt the professors were too cloistered and removed from reality. Truscott did not mingle with his fellow students. Unlike them, Truscott had to return to prison at night after classes.

In Ottawa, the Liberal government decided to let Truscott serve out his minimum sentence, then grant him parole.

In September 1968, Truscott applied for parole again. He had an unblemished prison record and Stienburg's help in putting together the necessary paperwork. By this point, Stienberg had changed jobs and was now working as a parole supervisor. In his application, Truscott made clear that he still maintained his innocence.

The parole board indicated they were favourably inclined to release Truscott, but suggested he might want to choose a new name so he wouldn't be hounded by reporters. There was also the question of where Truscott would live. It was risky to move in with one of his separated parents, given that is where the press would look for him first. Almost on a whim, Stienburg suggested Truscott could live at his house. Stienburg had a wife and two small children and no experience boarding ex-convicts, but he seemed keen.

In September 1969, the National Parole Board recommended that Truscott be given parole. Their recommendation went to the federal cabinet, where it was quickly approved.

On October 21, 1969, Truscott was released from the Collins Bay prison farm on parole into Stienburg's care. He was now a free man, albeit one with a false last name and a murder conviction on his record.

Chapter Nine: Freedom

Malcolm Stienburg did his best to ease his client back into mainstream life. Having spent a decade behind bars, Truscott wasn't used to making decisions for himself. Even simple things such as deciding what to order from a restaurant menu left him flustered and confused. With Stienburg's help, Truscott obtained a social insurance number under his assumed name. The ex-convict lived with the Stienburg family in Westbrook, a small community near Kingston, ON, and kept a very low profile.

Truscott soon attracted another devotee. Marlene, the teenager who had been so outraged by Truscott's case, sent him a Christmas card via Isabel LeBourdais. The author passed the card on, and, perhaps sensing a match in the making, arranged for Truscott and Marlene to chat over the phone. LeBourdais dropped by to visit Marlene at one point, with Truscott in tow.

In 1970, authorities moved Truscott to British Columbia, where he could live with his grandparents. By a twist of fate, Marlene had also gone west for the summer with a friend. Truscott began to visit Marlene at her Vancouver apartment. At first, the pair were just friends. Eventually, Truscott summoned the nerve to ask Marlene out on a date. Things progressed fast, and the two were soon in love. In the fall of 1970, Truscott and Marlene were married in a very private ceremony with no family or guests present (the couple feared a media onslaught if their nuptials became public knowledge).

The newlyweds moved back to Marlene's hometown of Guelph, ON. With his years of shop skills, Truscott got a job as a millwright (someone who repairs factory machines) in a plant called Linreed. He would work at this plant nearly 20 years. In the spring of 1971, Marlene gave birth to the pair's first child, a daughter named Lesley.

While Truscott did nothing to draw attention to himself, his case remained headline news. After his release, Truscott had spent a considerable amount of time in the company of journalist Bill Trent, a staff writer with *Weekend* magazine. Trent edited a series of interviews he did with Truscott into a book. Published in October, 1971, *The Steven Truscott Story*, made a strong case for the title subject's innocence.

Eight years later, Trent published a revised version of his book, entitled *Who Killed Lynne Harper?* This new edition was more of an investigative work and contained speculation on possible suspects besides Truscott.

By the time *Who Killed Lynne Harper?*, was published, Marlene and Steven had a son, named Ryan, in addition to daughter Lesley. By all accounts, Truscott was a good father and worker. Some of his co-workers and neighbours knew his real identify, but generally kept this information to themselves. In 1979, Dan Truscott died of cancer. One year later, Steve Truscott and Marlene had another boy, named Devon.

Even as he kept a low profile, Truscott had to deal with the burdens of parole and fame. In the eyes of the law, Truscott was still a convicted murderer. During his first years out of jail, he had to maintain contact with his parole officer and let him know whenever he was going to travel outside Guelph.

When she was 12 years-old, Lesley came across *The Steven Truscott Story*, in her school library. Steve and Marlene's daughter was familiar with the Truscott name from her father's relatives. To her astonishment, Lesley recognized some of these relatives in photographs accompanying the text. Two years after her discovery, Marlene told her daughter about Steven's true background. Lesley informed her mother she already knew. Eventually, Steven and Marlene also told younger son Ryan then Devon the truth.

In his spare time, Truscott rekindled his interest in mechanics. He purchased a motorcycle and loved to both ride it and tinker with it. The freedom of the road had an enormous appeal. Truscott also took flying lessons, thrilling to the sensation of being airborne.

The 1990s proved a tumultuous time for the Truscott's. In September 1994, Steve and Marlene's daughter, Lesley, got married in Guelph. And, for the first time in decades, Truscott sensed the faint possibility of finally clearing his name.

By the 1990s, testing for DNA—that is, the molecular

building blocks of life—became a common diagnostic tool in criminal investigations. Blood, hair, saliva, semen or skin could be tested for DNA to determine if there was a biological link between a suspect and victim. If a suspect's DNA was detected on a victim or at a crime scene, their guilt became all the more likely. The converse was also true; if a suspect's DNA could not be detected at a crime scene or on a victim's body, chances were the suspect was innocent.

In January 1995, DNA testing cleared Guy Paul Morin, of Queensville, ON, convicted of the gruesome murder of a young girl. It also cleared David Milgaard in July 1997, after he'd served 23 years for the murder of nursing aide Gail Miller in Saskatoon in 1969.

These cases galvanized the Truscott household. Could DNA testing exonerate Steven, once and for all?

Truscott became involved with a non-profit legal organization called the Association in Defence of the Wrongly Convicted (AIDWYC). Founded by lawyer James Lockyer in May 1993, this Toronto-based group seeks to rectify wrongful convictions. With Truscott's blessings, Lockyer set out to track down DNA from Lynne Harper.

Lockyer checked to see if the Center for Forensic Sciences (formerly the attorney-general's crime laboratory) had held onto any evidence from the Truscott case, such as Harper's clothing or tissue samples. The lawyer discovered, however, that all physical evidence connected with the Truscott case had been destroyed years before.

Undaunted, AIDWYC lawyers made formal requests with government authorities for information on Truscott's case.

Boxes and boxes of documents were delivered to the Truscott home in Guelph. Truscott's lawyers were given access to court transcripts and, for the first time, Crown records and notes made by police.

As AIDWYC's inquiry continued, the CBC-TV news program, *The Fifth Estate*, began its own investigation into the Truscott case. Butch George, Dr. John Addison and Dr. David Brooks all refused to be interviewed. One prominent figure who did take part in the documentary was Truscott himself. Truscott was taken back to Clinton, ON by the CBC-TV crew and interviewed at length.

The ensuing documentary, entitled "His Word Against History" was aired March, 2000. The documentary marked the first time Truscott had allowed himself to be interviewed on camera. *The Fifth Estate* also highlighted a previously unknown suspect named Sergeant Alexander Kalichuk. A known sexual offender and alcoholic, Kalichuk worked as a supply technician at RCAF Clinton from 1950 to August 1957. He transferred to another base, in Aylmer, ON in 1957, but frequently went back to Clinton, an hour's drive away.

Kalichuk had two convictions for indecent exposure in Trenton, ON from the early 1950s, and a serious problem with alcohol. Three weeks prior to Lynne Harper's death, on a farm road near St. Thomas, Kalichuk tried to lure a 10 year-old girl into his car with the promise of new underwear. When police arrested Kalichuk, they found a bag of panties and bottle of liquor in his car. Charged with contributing to the delinquency of a minor, the case against Kalichuk was eventually dismissed for lack of evidence.

Kalichuk was hospitalized with severe anxiety following

Harper's murder. He was eventually released but the military kept a close eye on him. He was a suspect in some incidents in the early 1960s involving a child molester in a car trying to pick up little girls around Exeter, ON. The CBC weren't able to ask Kalichuk about these incidents, because he died in 1975 after spending decades as an alcoholic.

In response to the CBC-TV documentary, Truscott's case was once again debated in the House of Commons.

Peter MacKay, justice critic for the Progressive Conservatives told the House on March 29, 2000, "The Truscott case as we know, has been a festering wound on the psyche of this nation and casts a shadow over the entire criminal justice system ... the case against Truscott was based on ambiguous, circumstantial and inconsistent testimony from children, impossible medical analysis of the murder victim and Mr. Truscott himself."

MacKay urged the ruling Liberal Party to do a full, public investigation into the case.

On May 16, 2000, AIDWYC lawyers and Truscott , held a press conference to announce they were doing a '690 review'. Section 690 (now 696) of the Criminal Code allows convicted people who have otherwise exhausted all other legal avenues to directly approach the justice minister and request a review of their case. Lockyer and two other AIDWYC lawyers, Marlys Edwardh and Philip Campbell, began to put together a report on Truscott's case.

Emboldened by all the support he was receiving, Truscott assumed his old last name. He explained why in an interview with CBC-TV's Peter Mansbridge on November 28, 2001.

"I want my kids to have my name, my dad's name," said Truscott.

One day after this interview, the federal justice minister received a detailed brief from AIDWYC lawyers that contained new evidence and pointed to other suspects besides Truscott.

On January 25, 2002, Ottawa announced that Fred Kaufman, a former judge with the Quebec Court of Appeal, would review Truscott's case. Kaufman, who had presided over an inquiry into the wrongful conviction of Guy Paul Morin, painstakingly read through thousands of pages of evidence. Kaufman ended up interviewing 21 people under oath, including Truscott himself.

Arnold "Butch" George and Jocelyne Gaudet were both subpoenaed to testify. During testimony on October 8, 2002, George said Truscott never asked that he lie for him. He was equally forthcoming about his own untruthfulness.

"Shit, we all lied," George told the judge in response to a question about lying during Truscott's criminal trial.

Gaudet, for her part, frequently swore during her testimony, claimed a bad memory and played down reports her original statements to police were motivated by an unrequited crush on Truscott.

Justice Kaufman submitted his four-volume, 700-page report on Truscott in spring, 2004. By this point, some of the major players in the Truscott saga, including Inspector Harold Graham, Isabel LeBourdais and Alexander Kalichuk were dead. Kaufman's report was received by Justice Minister

Irwin Cotler. In Kaufman's opinion, there was "a reasonable basis for a likely miscarriage of justice." Cotler agreed. On October 28, 2004, the justice minister asked the Ontario Court of Appeal to review Truscott's conviction.

On April 2006, the body of Lynne Harper was exhumed upon request of the Ontario attorney-general's office. The latter hoped to find DNA evidence on Harper's corpse that would settle the Truscott case. Unfortunately, forensic experts weren't able to collect sufficient DNA data because Harper's remains were in such poor condition.

On June 19, 2006, the Ontario Court of Appeal conducted a three-week hearing into the Truscott case. Representing Truscott's side were AIDWYC layers, Lockyer, Campbell and Edwardh.

This wasn't a new trial: the Ontario Court of Appeal was only allowed to hear new evidence. In spite of this restriction, the hearing represented Truscott's best chance in decades of conclusively proving he wasn't a murderer.

Chapter Ten: Vindication

Unlike Steven Truscott's 1959 trial, the most compelling witnesses to testify at the Ontario Court of Appeal review spoke for the defence.

On June 19, 2006, Dr. Michael Pollalen, Ontario's chief pathologist, testified that there wasn't enough evidence from Dr. John Penistan's autopsy to determine Lynne Harper's precise time of death. Trying to deduce time of death from stomach contents was "fraught with difficulty," said Dr. Pollalen, who also criticized Dr. Penistan for not taking photographs during his autopsy.

Some of the most damning testimony concerned Jocelyne Gaudet, star witness for the prosecution at Truscott's original trial. Under a different name, Gaudet had studied nursing in the 1960s. In June, 2006, Sandra Stolzmann, a nurse who roomed with Gaudet at St. Mary's Hospital in Montreal in the mid-1960s, had some interesting recollections. She told the court that Gaudet was terrified by the prospect of having to testify at the 1966 Supreme Court hearing into Truscott's case.

"She said, 'I lied and I can't go back and tell them,'" related Stolzmann.

Gaudet also said, 'Why are they going after Steven? Why were they going after Steven? They should have been going after the guy in the yellow car or yellow truck,'" Stolzmann recalled.

As it turned out, Gaudet never did testify at the 1966 Supreme Court review. Stolzmann said she passed her information about Gaudet on to police who apparently didn't do anything about it.

Another nurse, named Elizabeth Hulbert, backed Stolzmann. Hulbert had trained as an RN at St. Mary's Hospital between 1965 and 1968 and also knew Gaudet. She recalled that one evening the nurse trainers were talking about the Truscott case.

"The [Supreme Court review] of Steven Truscott was in the news or had just commenced at that time and this person across the room piped up and said, 'I was one of the witnesses at the Steven Truscott trial and I lied.' [Gaudet] admitted at that point that she had lied at the original trial," stated Hulbert.

Gaudet lied because she was jealous, reported Hulbert, presumably because Truscott wanted to spend time with Harper, not her. As Hulbert recalled, Gaudet told the nurse trainers, "I wanted to get at him.'"

On June 22, 2006, Hank Sayeau, by then a retired OPP superintendent, took the stand. He admitted that the OPP ignored its own guidelines during their investigation of Truscott.

Asked about police protocol in the 1950s about interviewing children, Sayeau said, "The general rule was that if they were of tender years, they had to be questioned or interviewed in the presence of their parents or guardian."

Sayeau admitted that police didn't seriously investigate other suspects beyond Truscott. In fact, police didn't even bother checking with other OPP detachments, Crown attorneys or the RCAF about known sex-offenders in the Clinton area.

Sayeau said he never investigated Sergeant Alexander Kalichuk because he didn't know who he was: "I didn't know the individual existed so I would never have been making any inquiries about him," the retired OPP superintendent told the Court of Appeal.

This confession stunned the judges, who seemed incredulous that police would focus all their attention on a clean-cut 14 year-old boy rather than known sexual offenders.

Justice Michael Moldaver asked Sayeau, "Did the thought ever cross your mind ... for someone to actually strangle [Harper] and then sexually assault her, you might want to be looking for someone who was more of a sexual pervert, a sexual psychopath? Did that ever cross your mind? Did you have a talk about that with your colleagues?"

"I don't think I did. I don't recall a conversation to that effect," Sayeau replied.

Truscott's old friend, Bob Lawson, finally got a chance to testify about his encounter with the strange car the night Harper disappeared. He said he reported the incident to the RCAF guardhouse but they didn't seem interested in following up. Lawson also repeated how Gaudet had approached him and asked him to change his testimony so his testimony matched hers.

A friend of Harper, meanwhile, testified how she and Lynne would hitch-hike all the time (in spite of her parents' later denial).

July 7, 2006, marked the last day of testimony. Renowned British pathologist Dr. Bernard Knight took the stand. Emeritus professor at University of Wales, consultant pathologist to the Home Office in the United Kingdom for 34 years, and author of several books, Dr. Knight was extremely critical of Dr. Penistan's methods.

'[Stomach content analysis] might be of some use to perhaps direct the police investigation early on and say well, 'I think she must have died within a few hours of the meal', but you cannot pin it down to any useful period of time in pinpointing the time of death. As I said, I've taught all my assistants, my post graduates, my students, that any doctor who gives a fraction of an hour in his estimate of time since death is either uniformed or incompetent," said Dr. Knight.

"Unfortunately, the media have fed this sort of public expectation of accuracy in all these endless programs that someone comes in and feels the brow of a corpse and says he died at 20 past 2:00 last Tuesday. That's utter nonsense; and the same applies to stomach contents," he added.

After all the witnesses and lawyers had been heard, the Ontario Court of Appeal contemplated their verdict.

When the Court of Appeal released their decision, on August 28, 2007, it was a legal bombshell: "In a decision released today, the court unanimously holds that the conviction of Mr. Truscott was a miscarriage of justice and must be quashed. The court further holds that the appropriate remedy in this case is to enter an acquittal. The court thus orders that Mr. Truscott should stand acquitted of the murder of Lynne Harper," read the official decision.

And with that, Canada's most controversial court case came to a close. Steven Truscott was acquitted. In the eyes of the law, he was no longer a convicted murderer.

The court made the obvious point that Harper's horrific death was "out of place with the actions of a 14 year-old schoolboy whose sexual advances were rebuffed by a 12 year-old classmate. Rather, this picture would appear to be the work of a sexual deviant for whom sex with a dead or dying child was somehow capable of providing stimulation."

The Court also discussed the importance of new medical evidence regarding stomach contents and rate of putrefaction.

"This fresh evidence significantly undermines the medical evidence relied on by the Crown in the prior proceedings to establish that Lynne Harper died before 8:00 pm on June 9, 1959 ... the time of Lynne Harper's death was a critical issue at trial and on the first Reference on the Crown's theory of the case, if Lynne Harper died between 7:00 and 8:00 pm, then the appellant must have killed her," stated the Court. "The court concludes that the fresh evidence relating to the time of death, considered in the context of the entirety of the evidence, could reasonably be expected to have caused the jury to at least have a reasonable doubt that Lynne Harper could have died before 8:00 pm. If the jury had a reasonable doubt on this factual issue, it could not have convicted the appellant."

Truscott received news of his acquittal on a cell phone, while driving with his family along Highway 401 near Milton, ON. According to *The Toronto Star*, Truscott took a call from his legal team then said, "Oh, that's fantastic. Fantastic."

"They finally got it right after all these years. I'm so used to fighting. Now we don't have to fight anymore," Truscott told *The Star*.

The decision wasn't a complete victory. Truscott and his lawyers had hoped the Court of Appeal would find him "factually innocent"—in other words, 100% exonerated. DNA testing, which might have found Truscott factually innocent, couldn't be used in his case, however.

Nonetheless, the acquittal was likely as close to closure as Truscott would ever get in the case. More was to come.

After the decision came down, Ontario Attorney General Michael Bryant publicly apologized to Truscott. Reporters quoted him as saying, "For that miscarriage of justice, on behalf of the government, I am truly sorry."

The hearing revealed there were more suspects in the Truscott case than anyone had known. One woman claimed that as a six-year-old child, she hid in her father's car. Her father went for a drive, stopped on a gravel road and carried the lifeless or limp body of a young girl out of the trunk and carried it to a grassy area. The girl's father was a minister and possible sexual offender who lived in Dungannon, ON, a village near the Clinton RCAF base. Another suspect, who had a conviction for rape in the Seaforth, ON area, was never questioned by police in the Harper case.

On July 7, 2008, the government of Ontario awarded Truscott $6.5 million in compensation.

"This is a bittersweet moment for us," said Steven and Marlene Truscott in a press statement. "When we began this journey more than a decade ago, we thought only of exonerating Steven—the possibility of compensation never entered our minds. Although we are grateful for the freedom and stability this award will provide, we are also painfully aware that no amount of money could ever truly compensate Steven for the terror of being sentenced to hang at the age of 14, the loss of his youth, or the stigma of living for almost 50 years as a convicted murderer."

About the only people upset by this compensation was the

family of Lynne Harper. Barry Harper, Lynne's brother, described the compensation to *The Globe and Mail* as "a real travesty." Barry further said he wouldn't tell Lynne's father, Leslie, who was very old and in a nursing home.

Sadly, while Steven Truscott and his family were finally able to close an extremely painful chapter, for the Harper family there would now be the lingering question of who really did kill their daughter, Lynne?

Epilogue

In late May, 2012, Steven Truscott was in the news again. This time, it was because he was ill with prostate cancer.

In an exclusive interview with author Julian Sher published in *The Toronto Star*, Truscott revealed the extent of his cancer treatment. He discussed his surgery (his entire prostate was removed in 2011) and extensive radiation therapy. Truscott appeared to be dealing with cancer in his usual stoic manner.

"Worrying about [my cancer] isn't going to make it go away. I figured if the government couldn't get rid of me, this wasn't going to get rid of me either," Truscott told *The Star*.

While the latest tests indicate the cancer hasn't spread, Truscott's battle has not been without cost.

"The surgery, radiation and stress over the past year have taken an obvious toll on Truscott. Once a strong, fit man with the ramrod straight bearing of a boy who grew up on an air force base, Truscott has put on weight, walks more slowly and lacks the energy he once had," stated *The Star*.

Not all was bad news, however: the piece mentioned that the Truscott family was living comfortably in an "expansive home on the outskirts of Guelph" purchased with some of $6.5 million in compensation the Ontario government paid out.

Made clear, however, was Truscott's desire for privacy. He has largely avoided the media since his stunning acquittal in 2007. Truscott politely declined an interview request for this book, for example.

The Truscott clan has used some of their newfound wealth to fund the Truscott Initiative in Justice Studies at the University of Guelph, a pair of scholarships for students working in the field of social justice. There are also plans to set up a chair in social justice studies at the same institution.

According to *The Star*, Truscott went public with his medical troubles to encourage men to get tested for prostate-specific antigen (PSA), a cancer indicator. The only other cause that would prod him back into the media spotlight, said Truscott, is capital punishment. Should the Canadian government attempt to bring back the death penalty—a punishment he strongly opposes—Truscott can be expected to become an activist once more.

"How many wrongful convictions have there been in Canada and how many of those people would be dead (under capital punishment)? I would come back for that," Truscott told Sher.

As for cancer, Truscott retains a touch of the genial cockiness he displayed as a boy, before his arrest.

"I've been given two chances," Truscott told *The Star*, referring to his reprieve from death row and the court ruling that overturned his conviction. "My cat has nine lives, so I have seven more to catch up."

Steven Truscott time line

January 18, 1945 – Steven Truscott born in Vancouver, BC to parents Dan and Doris Truscott

Summer 1956 – Truscott family moves to RCAF Station Clinton in Clinton, ON

June 9, 1959 – Around 7:00 pm, 14-year-old Steven Truscott encounters 12 year-old classmate Lynne Harper on the grounds of A.V.M. Hugh Campbell School, at RCAF Station Clinton. Truscott gives the girl a bike-ride to nearby highway. According to Truscott, Harper begins to hitch-hike, and is picked up by a car around 7:30 pm. Truscott bikes back to the school grounds and chats with acquaintances. Then he bikes home to be on time for 8:30 pm babysitting duties.

June 9, 1959 – Leslie Harper concerned his daughter hasn't returned home. Calls the RCAF guard house at 11:25 pm to report his daughter is missing.

June 10, 1959 – Lynne Harper has still not returned home. At 7:45 am, Leslie Harper goes to Truscott's house and asks if anyone seen Lynne. Steven Truscott replies in the affirmative.

Later that morning, police take Truscott out of class for questioning.

June 10, 1959 – Police go to Truscott household around noon to question Steven again, but he isn't home. Police return at 5:00 pm for more questioning. Police return again at 8:00 pm and ask Steven Truscott to retrace his movements from the previous night.

June 11, 1959 – Truscott is taken out of morning classes for more questioning by police. The police also interview other children at the school.

June 11, 1959 – At 1:50 pm, a search party of RCAF personnel find Lynne Harper's dead body on property belonging to Bob Lawson, a local farmer. Pathologist Dr. John Penistan arrives in the late afternoon to examine the body and death site.

June 11, 1959 – At 7:15 pm, Harper's body is removed from woods and taken to a Clinton, ON funeral home where Dr. Penistan and Dr. David Brooks (an RCAF base physician) perform an autopsy. Dr. Penistan says Harper likely died between 7:15 – 7:45 pm on June 9.

June 11, 1959 – OPP Inspector Harold Graham arrives in Clinton from Toronto, at 7:45 pm to head the investigation into Harper's death.

June 12, 1959 – Steven Truscott called out of class at 10:45 am to meet Inspector Graham. Truscott answers questions as a stenographer records his responses. Inspector Graham interviews several other children at A.V.M. Hugh Campbell School.

June 12, 1959 - Stomach contents from Lynne Harper taken

to attorney-general's laboratory in Toronto for analysis. According to Inspector Graham, the lab backs Dr. Penistan's time of death estimate. Inspector Graham orders police to pick up Truscott for more questioning.

June 12, 1959 – At 6:50 pm, police locate Truscott on the farm of Bob Lawson. Police take Truscott to the Goderich, ON, OPP station. Inspector Graham and other police interrogate Truscott. They believe he raped and murdered Harper, something Truscott denies. After a fruitless interrogation, police drive Truscott to the guard house at RCAF Station Clinton. Police arrive around 9:30 pm. Interrogation of Truscott continues.

June 12, 1959 – Daniel Truscott gets word that his son is at the guard house, races to see him at 9:40 pm. Doris Truscott arrives at guard house at some point during the evening. Police escort Doris Truscott back to her home and conduct a search with her permission. Dan Truscott grudgingly grants permission for a medical examination of his son.

June 12, 1959 - Truscott family physician, Dr. John Addison, arrives at the guard house at 10:30 pm to conduct examination of Truscott. He is assisted by Dr. David Brooks. Doctors find penile lesions on Truscott (which they believe are result of rape). After conducting the examination, Dr. Addison starts questioning Truscott.

June 13, 1959 – Early morning. Dan Truscott wants to take his exhausted son home, and let police resume their questioning later. Police, however, decide to arrest Truscott for the murder of Lynne Harper. Truscott is driven to Goderich, taken before a Justice of the Peace at 2:45 am and formally charged. Truscott then placed in a juvenile detention room in the Goderich courthouse.

June 13, 1959 – At 11:00 am, Truscott is arraigned before Juvenile Court Judge Dudley Holmes and is remanded to custody. Truscott is then placed in the Huron County jail in Goderich. A couple hours later, a funeral service for Lynne Harper is held in the Protestant chapel at RCAF Station Clinton.

June 19, 1959 – A young girl picking berries near Lawson's Bush finds Harper's gold locket, which had been missing.

June 29, 1959 – It is decided to hold Truscott's trial in adult court. This means he might face the death penalty if found guilty.

July, 1959 – The RCAF transfers Dan Truscott to a base near Ottawa, ON. Doris Truscott stays in a trailer near Goderich so she can be near her son.

July 13 – 14, 1959 – A preliminary hearing is held to determine if there is enough evidence to proceed with a trial for Truscott. It is decided there is.

September 16, 1959 – Steven Truscott trial begins in Goderich, ON. Truscott pleads not guilty. Dr. Penistan testifies that Harper died between 7:15 – 7:45 pm on June 9 and was killed in the same place her body was found. The trial features 74 witnesses, 77 exhibits and 11 days of testimony.

September 29, 1959 – Truscott's attorney, Frank Donnelly, gives his final address to the jury, pointing out that "there is no direct evidence which in any way links this boy with that murder" and that "there is some evidence that the girl was not killed in this bush."

September 30, 1959 – Jury deliberates briefly then find Truscott guilty, with a plea for mercy. The judge ignores this and sentences Truscott to death.

October 5, 1959 – *Toronto Star* columnist Pierre Berton publishes a column called, *Requiem for a Fourteen Year-Old*. In verse form, Berton questions the morality of hanging a 14 year-old. Berton receives reams of hate mail for his efforts.

October 10, 1959 – Lawyer for Truscott family appeals the verdict.

December 8, 1959 – Truscott's original execution date. The execution is postponed so Truscott's appeal can be heard.

January 12, 1960 – The Ontario Court of Appeal mulls over Truscott's conviction.

January 18, 1960 – Truscott turns 15. He is now scheduled to die on February 16, 1960.

January 20, 1960 – Ontario Court of Appeal dismisses Truscott's appeal.

January 21, 1960 – Federal government commutes Truscott's sentence to life in prison.

February, 1960 – Truscott begins serving his sentence at the Training School for Boys, a juvenile facility in Guelph, ON.

February 9, 1960 – Truscott lawyer files appeal to the Supreme Court of Canada.

February 24, 1960 - The Supreme Court turns Truscott's appeal down.

Early 1960s – Freelance writer Isabel LeBourdais investigates Truscott's case and decides he is innocent. No magazine in Canada will publish her story, however. She meets similar rejection when she expands her article into a book.

January 18, 1963 – Truscott turns 18 and is transferred to Collins Bay Penitentiary, a federal prison in Kingston, ON.

April 4, 1964 – Truscott applies for parole for the first time. His request is denied.

January 1966 – Isabel LeBourdais book, *The Trial of Steven Truscott*, is released in Great Britain. It is published in Canada two months later.

Spring 1966 – *The Trial of Steven Truscott* sells 60,000 copies in Canada in a few weeks and prompts questions about his case in the House of Commons.

April 1, 1966 – Harold Graham meets with high-ranking government and police authorities to denounce LeBourdais' book.

April 26, 1966 – Bowing to public pressure, the Liberal government announces it has referred Truscott's case for an unprecedented review by the Supreme Court of Canada.

May 19, 1966 – Dr. John Penistan writes what he calls an "agonizing reappraisal" of his autopsy results in which he dismisses his original, very precise estimate of the time of Harper's death. These findings are not revealed for decades.

October 5, 1966 – Two week hearing before the Supreme Court of Canada. Medical experts testifying on Truscott's behalf dismiss Dr. Penistan's time of death estimate and significance of Truscott's penile lesions. Truscott himself testifies (which he didn't do at his original trial). Truscott denies he killed Lynne Harper.

May 4, 1967 – Supreme Court votes 8-1 to uphold Truscott's conviction, with strong dissension from Justice Emmett Hall.

Spring 1967 – Dan and Doris Truscott separate.

Spring 1968 – Truscott transferred to Collins Bay prison farm, gets to work outdoors.

September 1968 – Truscott applies for parole again.

September 1969 – National Parole Board recommends Truscott be given parole. The recommendation is approved by the federal cabinet.

October 21, 1969 – Truscott released from jail into the custody of Malcolm Stienburg, a prison chaplain turned parole officer. Truscott still has a record for murder.

Spring 1970 – Authorities move Truscott to British Columbia. He makes the acquaintance of a young lady named Marlene who had been outraged by Truscott's conviction. The two fall in love and marry in a private ceremony that fall. The newlyweds decide to move to Guelph, ON (Marlene's home town). Truscott (using an assumed last-name) takes a job as a millwright.

1971 – Birth of Steven and Marlene's first child, Lesley.

Publication of *The Steven Truscott Story*, book based on interviews journalist Bill Trent conducted with Truscott.

1974 – Marlene and Steven Truscott have a son named Ryan. Truscott keeps a very low profile in Guelph, ON.

1979 – Dan Truscott dies of cancer

October 1979 – Bill Trent updates his 1971 book. The revised version, entitled, *Who Killed Lynne Harper?*, includes speculation on new suspects.

1980 – Steve and Marlene have third child, Devon, a boy.

September 1994 – Truscott's daughter Lesley gets married in Guelph.

1997 – Inspired by the example of Guy Paul Morin and David Milgaard (two men whose murder convictions were overturned when DNA evidence proved their innocence), Truscott contacts the Association in Defence of the Wrongly Convicted (AIDWYC), a legal non-profit group, in the hopes of being similarly exonerated.

Late 1990s – AIDWYC discovers all physical evidence connected to Harper case has long been destroyed. AIDWYC does succeed in getting the government to release a large reserve of documents relating to the Truscott case, many of which have never been seen by the public. CBC-TV begins working on a documentary about Truscott's case. Truscott agrees to be interviewed on camera for first time.

March 20, 2000 – CBC-TV airs its documentary on Truscott. Entitled, "His Word Against History", the documentary suggests Truscott was innocent and that Harper's real killer might have been an alcoholic RCAF airman with a fetish for young girls.

March 29, 2000 – Truscott case again debated in House of Commons.

May 16, 2000 – AIDWYC lawyers announce they plan to personally approach the federal justice minister for a review of Truscott's case.

October 2001 – A new book entitled, *Until You Are Dead* by Julian Sher makes a powerful case for Truscott's innocence.

November 29, 2001 – Minister of Justice receives an extensive brief from lawyers working for the Association in Defence of the Wrongly Convicted that offers new evidence in the Truscott case and points to other suspects.

January 25, 2002 – Federal government announces it will review the Truscott case. The review will be led by Fred Kaufman, a former judge with the Quebec Court of Appeal. Kaufman researches the Truscott case and hears testimony from witnesses.

2003 – Isabel LeBourdais dies.

Spring 2004 – Justice Kaufman submits a 700 page report on Truscott case to Justice Minister Irwin Cotler. Kaufman tells reporters there was "a reasonable basis for concluding that there was likely a miscarriage of justice."

October 28/2004 – Justice Minister Irwin Colter asks the Ontario Court of Appeal to review the conviction of Truscott.

April 2006 – Lynne Harper's body is exhumed to see if it can yield any DNA evidence. Her remains are too decomposed to offer any useable DNA.

June 19, 2006 – Ontario Court of Appeal holds a three week review of Truscott's conviction in which new evidence is revealed.

August 28, 2007 – Ontario Court of Appeal overturns Truscott's conviction and acquits him. He is no longer a convicted murderer. "In a decision released today, the court unanimously holds that the conviction of Mr. Truscott was a miscarriage of justice and must be quashed," reads the Ontario Court of Appeal statement. Ontario Attorney General Michael Bryant formally apologizes to Truscott on behalf of the province.

July 7, 2008 – The government of Ontario awards Truscott $6.5 million in compensation.

September 2009 – Blyth theatre festival in Ontario presents a play on Truscott, entitled, *Innocence Lost*.

May 21, 2012 – *The Toronto Star* announces that Steven Truscott is fighting prostate cancer.

List of Important Players

Steven Truscott: 14-year-old son of Dan and Doris Truscott

Dan Truscott: Steven Truscott's father

Doris Truscott: Steven Truscott's mother

Lynne Harper: 12-year-old classmate of Steven Truscott

Leslie Harper: Lynne Harper's father

Shirley Harper: Lynne Harper's mother

Jocelyne Gaudet: classmate of Steven Truscott and Lynne Harper

Arnold "Butch" George: friend of Steven Truscott

Douglas Oates: defence witness at Steven Truscott's trial

Richard Gellatly: defence witness at Steven Truscott's trial

Bob Lawson: Clinton area farmer

Constable Donald Trumbley: police officer

Gord Logan: defence witness at Steven Truscott's trial

Corporal Hank Sayeau: police officer

Dr. David Brooks: medical officer at RCAF base Clinton

Dr. John Penistan: pathologist for Clinton area

Inspector Harold Graham: leading police officer on Steven Truscott investigation

Dr. John Addison: the Truscott family doctor

John Funk: biologist at the Ontario attorney-general's laboratory

Dr. Noble Sharpe: physician at the Ontario attorney-general's laboratory

Judge Dudley Holmes: presiding judge at the preliminary hearing for Steven Truscott's case

Glenn Hays: Crown Prosecutor at Steven Truscott's trial

Frank Donnelly: defence attorney at Steven Truscott's trial

John Erskine: identification officer for Ontario Provincial Police

Philip Burns: prosecution witness at Steven Truscott's trial

Isabel LeBourdais: investigative journalist and author

Justice Robert Ferguson: presiding judge at Steven Truscott's criminal trial

Flying Officer Glenn Sage: RCAF officer who helped lead search for Lynne Harper's body

Dr. Elgin Brown: physician at the Ontario attorney-general's laboratory

Dr. Berkely Brown: physician who testified for defence at Steven Truscott's trial

Bill Trent: investigative journalist and author

John O'Driscoll: lawyer for family of Steven Truscott

Julian Sher: investigative journalist, TV producer and author

William Bowman: Crown Prosecutor at 1966 Supreme Court hearings

Ted Joliffe: defence lawyer at 1966 Supreme Court hearings

Arthur Martin: defence lawyer at 1966 Supreme Court hearings

Dr. Norman Wrong: physician who testified for defence at 1966 Supreme Court hearings

Dr. Francis Edward Camps: physician who testified for defence at 1966 Supreme Court hearings

Justice Emmett Hall: dissenting Supreme Court Judge in 1966 hearings

Malcolm Stienburg: prison chaplain and parole officer

Marlene Truscott: Steven Truscott's wife

Sergeant Alexander Kalichuk: suspect in murder of Lynne Harper

James Lockyer: lawyer, founder of the Association in Defence of the Wrongly Convicted (AIDWYC)

Justice Fred Kaufman: jurist who reviewed Steven Truscott's case

Irwin Colter: federal Justice Minister

Dr. Michael Pollanen: forensic pathologist who testified for defence at Ontario Court of Appeal hearings

Dr. Bernard Knight: physician who testified for defence at Ontario Court of Appeal hearing

Bibliography

Books

—LeBourdais, Isabel. *The Trial of Steven Truscott*. Toronto: McClelland and Stewart Limited, 1966.

—Sher, Julian. *"Until You Are Dead."* Toronto: Vintage Canada, 2001.

—Trent, Bill with Steven Truscott. *Who Killed Lynne Harper?* Ottawa: Optimum Publishing Company Limited, 1979.

Documents

-"Synopsis of Reference re: R v. Steven Murray Truscott." Ontario Court of Appeal judgement, August 28, 2007

—Kaufman Report, 2004. (http://www.cbc.ca/news/background/truscott/documents.html)

—"Magistrate's Court Preliminary Hearing." 1959. (http://www.cbc.ca/news/background/truscott/documents.html)

—Ontario Court of Appeal hearing, 1960. (http://www.cbc.ca/news/background/truscott/documents.html)

—Ontario Court of Appeal hearing, 2007 – 2008. (http://www.cbc.ca/news/background/truscott/documents.html)

—Superior Court of Ontario Trial, 1959. (http://www.cbc.ca/news/background/truscott/documents.html)

—Supreme Court of Canada hearing, 1966. (http://www.cbc.ca/news/background/truscott/documents.html)

—Supreme Court of Canada judgement, 1967. (http://www.cbc.ca/news/background/truscott/documents.html)

Periodicals

—"Belated Justice in Truscott Case." *The Toronto Star*, August 29, 2007.

—"Body Exhumed in Truscott Case." *The Toronto Star*, April 7, 2006.

—"Crown Opposes Evidence in Previous Hearings as 'Fresh' For Truscott Appeal, *Canadian Press*, May 25, 2006.

—"'Not Guilty' Not Enough for Truscott." *The Toronto Star*, August 28, 2007.

—-"Other Leads on Possible Suspects Ignored." *The Toronto Star*, August 29, 2007.

—"Poem Showed How the Case Inflamed Emotions From the Start." *The Toronto Star*, August 29, 2007.

-"Steven Truscott Wages New Battle for His Life." *The Toronto Star*, May 21, 2012.

—"'They Finally Got it Right.'" *The Toronto Star*, August 29, 2007.

—"Time to Right the Wrong Done to Steven Truscott." *The Toronto Star*, August 28, 2007.

—"Truscott Appeal Decision Expected Next Week." *Canoe News*, August 21, 2007.

—"Truscott DNA Tests Inconclusive." *The Toronto Star*, April 10, 2006.

—"With One Telephone Call, Weight of 48 Years Is Lifted." *The Toronto Star*, August 29, 2007.

—"Women Warrior's Aided Truscott." *The Toronto Star*, August 27, 2007.

Press Releases

—"Ontario Compensates Steven Truscott." Ministry of the Attorney General, July 7, 2008.

—"Steven and Marlene Truscott Respond to Attorney General's Announcement of Compensation." The Association in Defence of the Wrongly Convicted, July 7, 2008.

Television

—Steven Truscott interviewed by Peter Mansbridge, CBC-TV News, November 28, 2001. (http://www.cbc.ca/news/background/truscott/interview.html)

Websites

—Association in Defence of the Wrongly Convicted. (http://www.aidwyc.org/)

—Steven Truscott Timeline, CBC.ca, July 7, 2008. (http://www.cbc.ca/news/background/truscott/timeline.html)

—"The Search for Justice." CBC.ca, July 7, 2008. (http://www.cbc.ca/news/background/truscott/)

—"*The Steven Truscott Story*: Moment of Truth." CBC.ca, March 20. 2000, (http://www.cbc.ca/fifth/truscott/index.html)

—"*Until You Are Dead.*" Random House, (http://www.randomhouse.ca/features/steventruscott/home.html)

—"Victim's Family Stunned by Truscott Compensation." CBC.ca, July 8. 2008.

Acknowledgements

I wish to commend the Association in Defence of the Wrongly Convicted (AIDWYC) for their fine work in bringing justice to the unjustly accused. I want to thank Lorina Stephens at Five Rivers Publishing for bringing this book back from the dead and Jeanne Enright for being the world's finest neighbour and girlfriend.

About the Author

Nate Hendley is a Toronto-based journalist who has written a series of books, primarily in the true-crime genre. He lives with a very relaxed cat named Oswald and next-door to Jeanne Enright, world's finest girlfriend and neighbour. Nate's website is located at www.natehendley.com.

Books by Five Rivers

NON-FICTION

Al Capone: Chicago's King of Crime, by Nate Hendley

Crystal Death: North America's Most Dangerous Drug, by Nate Hendley

Dutch Schultz: Brazen Beer Baron of New York, by Nate Hendley

Motivate to Create: a guide for writers, by Nate Hendley

The Organic Home Gardener, by Patrick Lima and John Scanlan

Elephant's Breath & London Smoke: historic colour names, definitions & uses, Deb Salisbury, editor

Stonehouse Cooks, by Lorina Stephens

John Lennon: a biography, by Nate Hendley

Shakespeare & Readers' Theatre: Hamlet, Romeo & Juliet, Midsummer Night's Dream, by John Poulson

Steven Truscott, by Nate Hendley

FICTION

Immunity to Strange Tales, by Susan J. Forest

Growing Up Bronx, by H.A. Hargreaves

North by 2000+, a collection of short, speculative fiction, by H.A. Hargreaves

A Subtle Thing, Alicia Hendley

Kingmaker's Sword, Book 1 Rune Blades of Celi, by Ann Marston

Things Falling Apart, by J.W. Schnarr

And the Angels Sang: a collection of short speculative fiction, by Lorina Stephens

From Mountains of Ice, by Lorina Stephens

Memories, Mother and a Christmas Addiction, by Lorina Stephens

Shadow Song, by Lorina Stephens

88, by M.E. Fletcher

Stitching Butterflies, by Shermin Nahid Kruse

Western King, Book 2 The Rune Blades of Celi, by Ann Marston

Broken Blade, Book 3 The Rune Blades of Celi, by Ann Marston

Cloudbearer's Shadow, Book 4 The Rune Blades of Celi, by Ann Marston

King of Shadows, Book 5 The Rune Blades of Celi, by Ann Marston

Sword and Shadow, Book 6 The Rune Blades of Celi, by Ann Marston

Bane's Choice, Book 7 The Rune Blades of Celi, by Ann Marston

A Still and Bitter Grave, by Ann Marston

Diamonds in Black Sand, by Ann Marston

A Method to Madness: A Guide to the Super Evil, edited by Michell Plested and Jeffery A. Hite

5000 Mile Journey, by Kelly Stephens

Caliban, by Lorina Stephens

The Rose Guardian, by Lorina Stephens

YA FICTION

Mik Murdoch: Boy-Superhero, by Michell Plested

YA FICTION COMING SOON

Mik Murdoch: The Power Within, by Michell Plested

www.5rivers.org

CPSIA information can be obtained at www.ICGtesting.com
Printed in the USA
LVOW071731030113

314244LV00019B/916/P